Down Home with The Chief and Miss Maggie

by JIMMY BARTLE TAYLOR

DEDICATION

to my loving parents and family
and the Youth of America

Jimmy's favorite picture of her dad, H. Roe Bartle

CREDITS:

Roe Bartle's personal files

Margaret Jarvis Bartle

Richard Boehner, Pony Express Council
St. Joseph, Missouri

*"Trail to the Eagle — Six Decades of Scouting
in Kansas City — 1910–1970"*

Joseph E. Hunt
Seattle, Washington

Published by Leathers Publishing
3840 West 75th Street, Prairie Village, Kansas 66208

Printed in the United States of America
May 1995

For additional copies, write to Leathers Publishing,
3840 West 75th Street, Prairie Village, Kansas 66208 or
call (913) 384-6397 or fax (913) 384-5068.

ISBN 0-9646898-0-4

"H. Roe Bartle had many friends — each felt he was their best friend. Roe had a way of endearing himself to each person with whom he made contact."

Simon Rositzky – St Joseph, Missouri

"No matter how advanced in years he grew, however, adults often affectionately called him the biggest boy in Boy Scouts."

Star Magazine – July, 1991

"Chief was never too busy to challenge the best that is within us and to congratulate us on the awards earned. He brought encouragement and a helping hand to those in need of encouragement. And always kept an alert mind to the needs of those younger and weaker."

Eldon Newcomb – 1937

"What we Americans expect of our friends and our hero's too — is that they live so that what they do will live after them and that their memory will be a great one. This you have done and your careers, in scouting and in your beloved Kansas City, will be a memory for others to follow."

Byron Hunt – Seattle, Washington

"Even in poor health — he gave the speech of his life. He was the ultimate showman."

Alden Barber, Chief Scout Executive of USA

Contents

Handsome Chief in his 1930's Sea Scout uniform.

Introduction

By Joseph E. Hunt
Seattle, Washington

O n the evening of July 15, 1994, a number of us who had served on the summer camp staff of the Kansas City, Missouri Boy Scout Council during the thirties were witness once again to the power and strength and depth of the Bartle legend ... this for all of us, I am certain, the most dramatic and climactic demonstration of it.

The day had been hot and humid with occasional thunder showers, but the evening was not hot nor was it cool ... just perfect ... as I remembered evenings long ago in Lone Bear Council Ring. There is very little conversation as one walks to the ring. The oak forest is quiet, and there is a quiet anticipation and solemnity, for the inner circle of the Tribe of Mic-O-Say is forming. It had been unknown to us and unknown to her, but now they were inducting the daughter of the Chief into the tribe and had named her Lone Bear Princess.

The acclamation, applause was instant and electrifying. I have never in my life witnessed the equal of it. I have searched of adequately descriptive words ... thunderous, sustained, longest and strongest ever ... but these would not properly define it. There was a quality of joy, tribute and happiness over this wonderful thing that had happened. It was important to everyone there, regarding this place and time and that I am in the presence of the legend and tradition of Chief Lone Bear ... H.Roe Bartle ... the Bartle Legend and Heritage. I must somehow celebrate it. I applaud.

The applause finally subsided as Jimmy Bartle Taylor acknowledged it time after time. I was standing relatively close to Jimmy and moved to personally express my feelings of joy, for I was very much aware of the significance and meaning of the event for her. A line had formed to meet her, to talk to her, to hear her, all wishing to express their special feelings regarding this occasion. I waited, for these individuals were for the most part Scouts, young men and women, young leaders who had never known the Chief ... Roe Bartle.

I waited and listened. I heard what these young people said and asked, and with each a chill of emotion, a tingle running up and down the length of my being, and with each a vivid recollection of days when I had stood in the presence of the Chief, there at camp, in the inner circle of the Tribe of Mic-O-Say, and afterward as I read about him and heard from him now and then. These young people knew the legend and were aware of its significance ... there was an understanding of the heritage and tradition and challenge left by H. Roe Bartle, and now they were ... were actually ... actually meeting, talking with and hearing from his daughter.

They listened, too, and I also listened to her responses as she reached out to each one ... responding to each one, and they found this was not simply a matter of being in the presence of the Chief's daughter, but rather they now through her knew him, because Jimmy Bartle Taylor radiates what he was, and she makes the heritage live. They sensed this. They knew this. This, the power and strength and depth of the legend.

There are many other manifestations of it ... the Bartle Convention Hall in Kansas City ... the heroic statue in the lobby of the hall ... the council camps bearing his name ... Lone Bear Council Ring ... American Humanics ... the impact of his personality, character and leadership on the host of organizations and institutions he led and served.

There is, of course, a story connected with any individual who has left such a mark as his. Jimmy Bartle Taylor tells this interesting and fascinating story of her parents, Roe and Margaret Bartle, for she was very, very much a part of it, supporting, encouraging, sustaining, filling in for him, and yet leading a full life of her own, pursuing a great variety of challenging pursuits and activities of service. Jimmy takes you back to the immigration of Sam Bartle from England, his marriage to Ada ... these are the parents of Roe. She relates the assignments of Sam, the Presbyterian minister. There are some of us who remember the Reverend Bartle when he was the minister of the church we attended in St. Joseph, Missouri. He was a dynamic person. One could see this, and one could judge that Roe was very much like him. Jimmy takes you through the years when Sam and Ada were rearing him, and that I suspect was no easy task. There is the sequence in which Roe decides to join the army. He was always large for his age and enlisted at age 13. Dr. Bartle had to go down and get him "de-enlisted."

There were the years at Fork Union and Chattanooga, and those of us who had the privilege of serving on the staff at camp heard Roe sing the fight songs of each … with his superb singing voice … it was superb not only for singing but for speaking. I have seen him push aside the microphone in a great hall and say, "I don't need this." And he didn't; he could fill the hall without it … as his message would uplift and motivate and inspire. To campers at Osceola he would close the campfire with his "big idea" … we would hear this and learn about what is right and the demands of character and responsibility and leadership, and taking part and doing, as he stressed the principles and moral values of Scouting. There could have been no one listening whose life was not strongly impacted. This was a gigantic role model.

You will find there was a number of career opportunities or avenues Roe Bartle considered. Those of us who have in some manner shared his past are grateful he went out to Wyoming to assume the Scout Executive role for the state. He brought boundless youth and enthusiasm to it. In addition, most likely the greatest correlation of achievement resulted not only from his energy, but from a highly developed sense of creativity and the ability to recognize conditions and factors that would help him attain his objectives. Scouting was very young in those days. He saw the potential of it and realized that there must be not only challenges to youth, but recognition of excellence and achievement as well. It was a fortunate thing when he met and got to know the Indian chief, Lone Bear. Lone Bear shared with him some of the rituals and traditions of his tribe, and Bartle, as a result, conceived and planned for an opportunity to establish the Tribe of Mic-O-Say as an honorary organization for Boy Scouts who established a continuing record of excellence at camp. Perhaps this organization had more to do with the future direction of his life than any other factor.

Jimmy recounts a charming story of the courtship of Margaret. She had told him that she would consider marrying him when he had permanently embarked upon a career. He did this when he went to Wyoming, and they were married, and she followed him back. She thusly became another important key factor in the achievements and marks that have created the Bartle legend.

We read of the move to Saint Joseph, Missouri, as the Scout Executive, and thence to Kansas City. Wherever Roe Bartle had been, he had shown unheard-of increases in boy membership, volunteer leadership recruitment, exceptional gains in the number of Scouts attending summer camp, and in the creation of new and exciting programs, events and activities that appealed to the imagination of Scout-age youths and attracted them to membership. The national office of the Boy Scouts of America recognized this and spread his ideas and programs throughout the movement. I am certain there are many of us who have been involved for many years in Scouting know that there is no individual who has had nearly as much to do with the growth and development of the Boy Scout program as H. Roe Bartle. This is true not only because of the pace and path he set in the Kansas City Council, but because of the staff he developed there ... the staff he recruited, and whose imagination he captured. He was their mentor. Many of them became Scout Executives in other councils. As time went along, they trained others who became Chief Scout Executive ... the Bartle tradition still lives today through these generations for which he was the initial spark. And all of that is not to mention the young men who were Scouts under his dynamic influence. They are leaders in Scouting and other fields across the land, even today. Here is the legend ... the influence remains strong.

There were aspects of the thirties which were adverse ... very much adverse to the moral values Bartle was instilling in young men along with high standards of responsible participation and citizenship involvement they had learned at camp and in other Scouting programs. It was a group of Mic-O-Says who came to him and expressed their concerns about the city government of Kansas City and prevailed upon him to run for Mayor. He did so and thus moved onto the local scene ... the state scene ... the regional scene ... the national scene, and his influence and dynamism went out to the world. Jimmy tells us the story of Mr. Mayor and the First Lady. It was a whole new world. Margaret became Miss Maggie and made speeches and appearances for him when his schedule did not allow him to attend.

Jimmy's parents had always been busy, always involved, and taking on key roles and challenges. She tells us of growing up in this hectic, but loving environment ... of the marvelous days and experiences at the ranch ... the good life as she identifies it ... and the cherished camaraderie that was developing between her and her father. She tells us of the birth of her and Jimmy Taylor's daughters and how living within the growing legend caused not only opportunities, but problems for the family as well. She relates the war years and the impacts on the family and Bartle's impact on the scene. Jimmy asks near the end, "Where have the years gone?" She has treated that ... you will marvel at the scope of this life ... you will shed some tears, and you will be exhilarated by the fascinating story of these people's lives that has resulted in a legend, a heritage and legacy that remains strong today. And you will know in reading it that the daughter is in truth the daughter of H. Roe Bartle, and she is carrying the torch and spreading his spirit. You would marvel if you could but see her captivating the Boy Scouts of today on the Bartle Reservation ... relation to them ... leading them in song. The Chief is there.

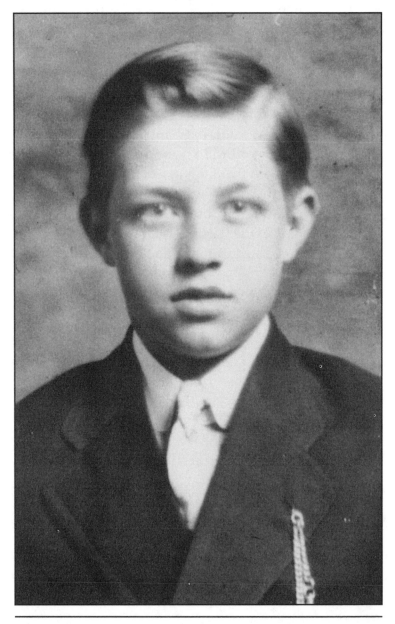

Young Harold at age nine. At age 15, he decided he would be called by his mother's maiden name, Roe.

In the Beginning

n 1887, at the age of 16, a young man by the name of Samuel Dunn Bartle crossed the Atlantic from the United Kingdom to the United States. He wanted to seek a more challenging and meaningful future and broaden the scope of his life. Sam worked hard putting himself through college and the seminary, and in the years to follow acquired his Doctor of Divinity degree. He saved what money possible and in time purchased passage for his mother and sister to come to this great new land of which he had now become a citizen.

Being somewhat of a circuit rider in the early years of his ministry, he had the good fortune of crossing the path of Ada Mae Roe, the daughter of a well known and admired Illinois physician, Dr. Malcolm Roe. Sam was greatly attracted to this charming and beautiful young lady with an aristocratic background and became very much infatuated with her. He soon fell deeply in love with Ada and begged for her hand in marriage, for he knew she would always be the only love for him. Ada's family was very displeased. They really did not want their beautiful daughter marrying a poor immigrant minister who never could, in their opinion, realize a satisfactory financial future. Love and persistence, however, conquered all. Ada and Sam were united in marriage at five o'clock, Wednesday evening, November 24, 1897, in Chana, Illinois. After December 20, they would be at home in Oasis, Iowa. Through this great union a son was born on June 25, 1901, weighing 10-1/2 pounds. They named this hefty boy Harold Roe Bennett Sturdevant Bartle. Ada's family had somewhat disowned her for marrying Sam, but this young son had winning ways from early childhood and won their hearts over, and thus the family was united with good feelings all around.

Harold Roe Bennet Sturdevant Bartle in his Christening dress.

Ada Mae Roe Bartle with her pride and joy, Harold — her only child.

The Early Years

In 1910 young son Harold and his mother accompanied Sam aboard a ship for the United Kingdom. While there, they not only visited relatives but also saw the sights of London. Harold absorbed everything he saw and heard … a characteristic that was clearly evident throughout his life. His outlook was already beginning to broaden.

Harold had only one pet as a child, medium size ol' yellar, named "Buck." He dearly loved this dog. When you saw Harold, you saw Buck, and when you saw Buck, you saw Harold. One afternoon when Harold came out of the schoolhouse, Buck was not there waiting for him. Harold ran home as fast as he could to see what ol' Buck was up to, but the dog was not to be found. Harold was devastated and asked his mother if she had seen Buck. It was his mother who had to break the news to him that his dog had died while Harold was in school, and his father had held a burial ceremony for him. Harold could not accept this news and dashed up to his room where he hid himself in the closet until the next day. He had lost his friend, and even his parents could not get him to come to dinner. Harold was completely crushed, and this was the last pet in the family until he brought one home for his daughter. We will relate to this later on.

Harold was not one to play very much, perhaps because he was an only child and excelled in all he did. He had a very inquisitive and inquiring mind which remained so the rest of his life. Being a PK (preacher's kid), Harold observed much about his surroundings plus the manner in which the various members of the congregation conducted their lives. Sam's calling to a church in Norton, Virginia, expanded this awareness and gave Harold the opportunity to grow up and learn more about people in the coal mining country of southwest Virginia.

The Bartle family was very musical. Sam had a strong singing voice, and Ada had one of operatic quality and was a master of both organ and piano. Harold learned to play all the wind instruments, the pipe organ and piano. Playing the organ and piano had come easy to Harold, and at the age of 13 he was playing the organ each Sunday for church services. He, however, felt he was too big to be doing such, and therefore one Saturday afternoon went to the barber shop and told the barber to shave his head. He felt for sure his parents would not want him sitting up in front of all the congregation playing the organ, at least until after his hair grew out once more ... and hopefully

Samuel Dunn Bartle — father of Roe Bartle — November, 1897

nevermore! The barber inquired if his parents had given him permission for the "haircut," and Master Harold assured him there was no problem, all was okay. After having had his head completely shaved, he left the barber shop proud and happy. He felt he would no longer be teased by all the fellows for playing the organ every Sunday. Upon his arrival home, things quickly changed. His mother was completely horrified. His father was thoroughly disgusted. The tables had turned. His punishment turned out to be playing the organ for everything that was scheduled throughout the summer months at the church. He was thankful that his hair grew out once again in a few weeks, and, needless to say, he was embarrassed enough that he never tried that sort of trick again.

At that same age of 13, Harold enlisted in the army! He lied about how old he was. Being tall and large for his age, he was able to get away with this, and there wasn't any reason not to believe him. Learning of his son's latest endeavor, Sam secured proof of his age and was able to get his son discharged in a few days.

Harold spent his summers with his grandparents in Illinois until about the age of 15. He learned a great deal from his grandfather, Dr. Malcolm Roe. He would go with the doctor in his buggy as he made his calls. His favorite uncle, Dr. John Roe, would also take him on house calls and, as a result, Harold became very knowledgeable in the medical field at a very early age. He was not yet 15 when there was an occasion that required his knowledge. The doctor was off on an emergency call and was not available when a young woman was ready to deliver her baby. Harold felt there was only one thing to do at this point; he rushed to the lady's side and delivered the baby like a pro.

Times were hard in the early 1900s — especially for ministers. Harold grew so fast his wardrobe never fit properly. A greater part of his early life found him wearing clothes donated by the parishioners. Shirt sleeves were too short and his pants too tight as well as too short. He made a pledge to himself that once he was out on his own, he would never again wear hand-me-down clothes. He lived up to that vow. For the most part his clothes were tailor made after he left college.

Cadet Years

At the age of 15 Harold decided he did not want to be called Harold any longer. He told his parents from this time forward he wanted to be called by his mother's maiden name, Roe, and informed them he would no longer answer to the name of Harold. He could not imagine the girls cheering him on at a football game yelling, "Come on, Harold, run, Harold, run, Harold." Nonetheless, most of his relatives continued calling him Harold (except for his understanding parents), until after he was married. I was six or seven years old when we were visiting some family relations, and I had heard them calling dad Harold all evening. When it was time for me to go upstairs to bed. I got halfway up the stairs, turned around and said, "Good night, Harold." They all laughed. Even Dad thought it was funny, and the expression on my face told it all. Therefore, we shall refer to Harold as Roe for the remainder of his life.

Chicken every Sunday was a true and common saying in the early 1900s. When members of the church invited the minister and his family to dinner on Sunday,

At the age of thirteen, Roe Bartle tried to enlist in the service.

it was always chicken. When contributions could not be placed in the collection plate, members would bring food to the manse. It was usually chicken, eggs and, during the season, fresh vegetables. At the age of 16, Roe informed his parents he had eaten the last chicken and eggs he would ever eat. He felt he had already consumed a lifetime quota of each, and he kept that vow to his dying day. No more chicken and chicken derivative!

While living in Norton, Virginia, Roe had worked in the coal mines during the summer months when he was on vacation from high school. This experience was also a help to his family before his entrance to Fork Union Military Academy as a freshman in 1916. It was a fortunate choice for his schooling, as it developed him from a timidly rebellious boy to a debater, football player and campus leader with a high sense of loyalty, honor and achievement. He excelled in all he did in life. His high school records prove his accomplishments.

The 1918 *Skirmisher,* the school yearbook, listed his activities during his sophomore year: treasurer of the sophomore class, treasurer of the Glee Club, member of the Southwest Virginia Club, member of the Ciceronian Literary Society, member of the Snead Hall Club, member of the R.A.P. Club, and on the Finance Committee of the Y.M.C.A.

The 1919 *Skirmisher,* his junior year, lists the following activities: secretary of the junior class, Cadet Captain of Band Company, advisor to the Athletic Association, secretary of the Glee Club, president of the Wise County Club, president of the Ciceronian Literary Society, and secretary of the Southwest Virginia Club.

The 1920 *Skirmisher,* his senior year, listed the following: editor of the *Skirmisher,* secretary/treasurer of the

Athletic Association, Cadet Major and Battalion Commander (the leader of the Cadet Corps), president of the Ciceronian Literary Society, secretary of the Science Club, vice president of the Hatcher Hall "Roughnecks," secretary of the Y.M.C.A., winner of the "Best Orator" award and voted "Best All-Around School Man." The dual drive for success had set his course. He attended Fork Union for four years, graduating with honors in 1920.

During his sophomore year in 1918, Roe had one of the most important experiences of his young academic life. Colonel N.J. Perkins, the headmaster, was Roe Bartle's debate teacher and early on scheduled Roe for a debate. The idea of his first debate was a terror for Roe. He felt he could never do this assignment. It frightened him to the point where he took refuge under the bed in his room. He did not go to class or show up that evening at the scheduled time for the debate. A search went out for young Bartle, and Colonel Perkins happened to be the one who found him. He pulled him out from under the bed and marched him by the collar to the podium in the auditorium. Much to Roe's amazement, he won the debate with flying colors. You might say this was the beginning of his speaking career. From that time on he was on the school's debating team, and they always won over the other schools. People who knew Roe later in life could hardly imagine him being so shy, and Roe thanked the Colonel many, many times in the years that followed for his understanding, patience and fortitude.

I should add that the experience at Fork Union was a family affair. Major Samuel Dunn Bartle, Ph.D. and D.D., in 1919 was Commandant and the instructor in history and military science at Fork Union Military Academy. He was also pastor of the local Presbyterian Church. Ada Roe Bartle taught English and penmanship and was an honorary member of the "Ministerials."

Higher Education

Roe decided upon pursuing his education at the University of Chattanooga where he intended to study law. This was something new for the family. All of the men on his mother's side were doctors, while those on his father's were ministers of the gospel. Ada, however, had prayed that her son Roe could follow in his father's footsteps as a minister. She also reckoned that he might have a career in opera, for even without training, he had a strong, rich and beautiful baritone singing voice. She had been pleased to know he was sharing his talent with others as he sang at clubs, organizations, parties, churches and choirs. But at this time, Roe had decided upon a law degree.

Characteristically, Roe did most anything he could at Chattanooga to make money to pay for his education. He tended the furnace for his room, mowed the grass and cleaned the windows. He even took on a news reporter's graveyard beat, wherein his first assignment for the *Chattanooga Times* was to cover a big fire where several buildings burned. In his column he told about the scope of the fire, colorful flames and crumbling buildings, but in the very last line he wrote, "A man was killed." This, of course, should have been the headline. Thus, in his first assignment he learned an important lesson in not only writing for a newspaper, but established a long-time ability of putting important things first.

This was an all-American young man. In addition to

his earning the money to pay for his education, he played fullback on the university football team. I might add that he paid a price for indulging in this sport. Due to his ankles being broken several times in high school and college football, he had to wear high top shoes for the rest of his life. I really have no idea, considering all he did at school, when he ever had time to study, but he finished at the university with academic honors.

One evening while in Chattanooga, Roe had just finished mopping a restaurant floor and was on his way home when he was stopped in his tracks by a robber. The robber took his rings, watch, money and billfold. As the robber was about to leave, Roe asked him, "What does that pocket watch mean to you?"

The robber replied, "Nothing, why?"

"Well, it means the world to me as my grandfather gave it to me, so why don't you just give that back to me and you can have the rest." Roe was astonished as the robber complied. Roe continued his way back to his quarters feeling very pleased with himself and proud that he had saved a family heirloom.

Decisions for the Future

In 1920 Sam Bartle received a calling to the Presbyterian church of Lebanon, Kentucky. Roe proceeded there from Chattanooga and began working in the law offices of Sylvester Russell. At the same time he was continuing to study law through the Hamilton College of Law, a mail order school in Chicago, and received his Doctor of Jurisprudence degree in 1921. It is difficult to believe that this man ever had any spare time, but while in Lebanon he coached the high school baseball team and served as umpire. He also coached the high school football and basketball teams ... spare time!

All of these activities seem to belie one of the main reasons he had come to Lebanon. It was doctor's orders. Roe had suffered pneumonia and nearly died. The doctor told him he must take life easy for at least a year to regain his health.

But I guess the type of things he was now pursuing were of a less hectic and stressful nature. During this time he became choir director of his father's church and also formed a choral group that performed for many programs throughout the area.

Now in addition he took on perhaps the most meaningful activity that would determine the fundamental purpose of his future life. He because the Scout leader of the only Boy Scout troop in Lebanon. It was clear he was becoming a leader in the community. The enthusiasm he brought to all the roles he carried, his winning ways with people of all ages, his devotion to his parents and his God; these were the foundation for his receiving the opportunity to join the early ranks of professional Boy Scouting.

Margaret Jarvis Bartle was called Miss Maggie by family.

Miss Maggie

After three sons and one daughter, Granville Jarvis and his wife Margaret Mae Finch Jarvis had a second daughter, Margaret Ann Carlene, born in Jessamine County, Logana, Kentucky, on August 14, 1904. Granville made a living for his family by tending one of the finest peach orchards in the territory plus growing tobacco.

Granville had a younger sister, Lillian Mae, who had married a wonderful gentleman by the name of James Minor Rains, 20 years her senior. The two wanted children, but after several years of trying, Lillian remained barren. When Margaret Ann Carlene was three years old, her Aunt Lillian went to Granville and asked if she and her husband James could take Margaret Ann and rear her as their own since they had no children. These were the days when one would not have given up a son as they could help with the heavy chores, but it was felt girls could do little or nothing, and therefore Granville complied with the wishes of his sister. He told Lillian to go upstairs and pack all of Margaret's clothes and take her home to Lebanon, Kentucky ... wishing her happy days ahead. It was not until dinner time when Margaret Mae Jarvis rang the dinner bell that the family noticed that Margaret Ann had not come to the table for dinner. It was at this point that Granville announced to the family, including his wife, that he had given Margaret Ann to his sister Lillian who had asked to raise her since they had no children. Margaret Mae lived to be in her 70s, and she never got over the fact that Granville had given one of her precious children away without even discussing the matter with her.

New Home — New Name

Lillian and James were elated over the addition to their family. They were very proud of their newly acquired daughter. Although Margaret was never legally adopted by James and Lillian, she went by the name of Margaret Rains from that time forward. All of her school records and diplomas identified her as Margaret Rains.

Being a natural daughter and also "adopted" made for a different lifestyle for Margaret. Lillian was very jealous and really did not like to share Margaret with her natural brothers and sisters. Nonetheless, Margaret managed to go for visits during the summer months. This caused family problems as she was always dressed beautifully and had everything she could ever want, whereas her brothers and sisters had little or nothing. In time, there were four blood brothers and three sisters. She dearly loved her mother, but could never come close to her father. He was not an easy person to understand, to know or love.

Margaret's parents had purchased a farm outside Danville, Kentucky, and when she was older, she spent more time out on the farm with her brothers and sisters. She learned how to thin corn, pick cherries, strawberries, green beans and cucumbers, and to care for all the things one grows in a large family garden. She particularly loved the prize peaches plus several kinds of apples that were grown, along with three kinds of grapes. Concords were her favorite. She would stand under the vines and eat these grapes until she was almost sick. Even though milking the cows was the boys' job, she kept after them until they let her learn how to milk.

It was the job for Margaret and her younger sister, Ruth, to churn and make butter. At times the two would be exhausted before the butter came. She and her sisters, Georgia and Ruth also had the duty of doing the dishes. All was not work, however, as the three girls got to spend some time each year in Lexington, Kentucky, with their Aunt Myrt and Uncle Frank who did not have children. There were good times going to the movies, swimming and teenage parties. Uncle Frank was constantly providing them ice cream and candy.

Uncle Frank was a contractor and constructed many of the buildings still standing today in Lexington, Kentucky, including the courthouse. There were many adventures for Margaret while visiting in Lexington. She was eight or nine when Uncle Frank brought home one of the first big cars, a Pierce Arrow. While on the subject of cars, I should add when she was 13, James Rains got a seven-passenger Studebaker. She and Lillian had driving

50th anniversary — Granville and Margaret Mae Finch Jarvis — parents of Margaret Bartle.

lessons at the same time.

A year later, at 14, Margaret weighed only 85 pounds. Apparently the growth hormones took effect, and she grew so fast her clothes had to be altered nearly every week. Her doctor ordered her to rest each afternoon, and because she liked him very much, she did as he requested even though she was bored. I suspect she felt very close to the doctor because he had removed her tonsils, sewed her chin and elbow (resulting from falls) several times and brought her through pneumonia twice.

Over half the population of Lebanon was Catholic, and Margaret would occasionally go to Mass with her friends. Father Hogerty, the parish priest, was generally loved by everyone, including Margaret. He remained in Lebanon for 50 years by a special dispensation from the Pope, and always remained in Margaret's memory but, of course, her aunt and uncle were Methodist, and she attended church with them each Sunday.

She had the good fortune of growing up in a happy home. They made their own fun most of the time. She dearly loved to roller skate, walk on stilts, ride bicycles, swim, ride horseback, and looked forward to birthday parties. Halloween was always a special fun night. All the children dressed in costumes and went door to door. There were times, however, when porch furniture found its way down the street. In some neighborhoods the outhouses were tipped over, and one year a cow was taken upstairs in the schoolhouse to the principal's office. That was really a mess. I don't know if any of the "villains" were apprehended.

In high school Margaret played running guard on the basketball team. Her team was good, and they won nearly all their games. In those days they wore black bloomers instead of shorts to play their games.

Virginia was one of Margaret's best friends. Virginia's father was the minister of the Presbyterian church in Lebanon. When he was transferred elsewhere, the manse in Lebanon soon became the home of Sam and Ada Bartle. Sam united the two Presbyterian churches during the three years the family spent in Lebanon. Sam was a marvelous speaker. All the young people loved to hear him, and many would come from the other churches to listen to his Wednesday night services.

The Introduction

Lebanon was a small town of about 5,000, and everyone knew everyone else. Margaret, however, being away at a boarding school had never met the new Presbyterian minister's son. He was never there when she was home during vacation. At the end of the year she attended a high school class program one evening, and it just must have been in the cards, as who should come in and sit beside her but Roe Bartle. After observing the situation, Lillian and James leaned forward and introduced her to Roe. At the conclusion of the program, Roe asked to walk her home. On the way they stopped at Humphey's, the "hangout," where they had an ice cream soda and a milk shake.

A few days later, a friend down the street in the next block invited Margaret to a party and told her that Roe Bartle would be her date. She could not remember if she was thrilled or not. She did recall her aunt took her to the dressmaker who made her an aqua-colored taffeta dress. She felt most particularly dressed up for the party, as she was so frequently dressed in middy suits and gym bloomers for basketball. Roe brought her a corsage. It was her first, and she was thrilled.

After that party, she and Roe had many dates, especially during the week of Chautauqua... always the highlight of summer. Looking to the future, Roe was practicing law, and that spring he had filled in as teacher for the seventh grade. He was thinking about careers, but during Chautauqua he usually ate picnic supper with Margaret's family between the day and night programs. The day programs were usually lectures, and the night ones were plays or musicals like "Poor Butterfly" and the "Mikado." Therefore Margaret and Roe saw a lot of each other that week and really for the rest of that summer.

Back in those days there were, of course, no radios, TV or videos; yet there was much to do. The young people made their own fun. They played a lot of games, went swimming, tennis, horseback riding, played baseball and croquet. They double-dated a lot. Taking walks was popular, especially on Sunday, out to the park or in the woods. There were all kinds of things to keep Margaret busy at home, such as learning to cook, sewing, embroidery, tatting, hair pin lace, piecing quilts and smocking. When she was younger, she made doll clothes. Hands were seldom idle.

When there was a fire, especially at night, everyone always turned out to watch. The worst fire Margaret could remember was when the livery stable burned. They were unable to rescue the horses, and it was a horrible sight seeing all those horse bodies the next day. Another fire was a hotel in Lebanon, but fortunately no one was killed.

There was the old opera house where the great minstrel shows of the day were performed. Companies would come and put their shows on as a money raising project for P.T.A. or other organizations. They would often seek local talent, and Margaret would do the "cake walk" in which she always carried a red parasol. She also danced and was great in speaking parts, but was unable to carry a tune. She always regretted she could not be in the choir, chorus or other singing groups with her friends.

Not to be outdone, Roe was in a play where he took the part of a female "Tootsie Wootsie." To fit the role, he borrowed a dress from one of the larger ladies in town. The part required that he faint in his lover's lap. When he did, the dress split right down the back. It broke the audience up. He had only shorts and undershirt on underneath the dress. The faint was supposed to be funny, but it was funnier seeing him trying to get off the stage without losing the dress.

Roe again took the role of coach. He coached the high school baseball team and was umpire for the Lebanon team. Before the games with the nearby towns, he always brought his watch and billfold to Margaret to hold during the game. That thrilled her, as it would any teenager.

Margaret stayed home after the year at boarding school, as she wanted to be with her classmates for her senior year of high school. Roe also stayed in Lebanon practicing law with Sylvester Russell, as that was the year he was to take life easy after nearly dying from pneumonia.

When Margaret graduated from high school that year, she won a medal for the "best reader." Her selection was "The Maid of France." It was about as long as a one-act play and probably was the start of her "stage career."

That summer after graduation from high school, Virginia came to visit for a couple of weeks. One was Chautauqua week. There were lots of parties, swimming

Margaret Bartle — summer visit to Kentucky — 1924

and picnics. When it was time for Virginia to go home, she begged Lillian to let Margaret go home to Henderson, Kentucky, with her for a few weeks. Lillian consented and, of course, the visit to Virginia's started off with lots of parties. Margaret had not felt very well for three days but did not give up on all the activities, as she thought she was just tired from all the fun that was going on and the late hours. However, at a swimming party she tried to swim across the pool and had to give up. When she got back to the house, they took her temperature and it was 104. She was put to bed immediately, and Virginia's mother called the doctor at once. Well, of all things, she turned up with diphtheria. The doctor gave her 80 units of antitoxin even before the culture came back. It was a good thing he had not waited, as he had to give her more after receiving the culture report. They felt she was going to die. The doctor had them call her aunt and uncle to tell them how seriously ill she was. All in the house were quarantined, except the Reverend, who had to move out. Everyone who had been with Margaret had to be given shots. The pool at the country club where she had been swimming had to be drained and disinfected. It was no doubt a relief to the family when she was well enough to return home. She always remembered how good they were to her and that Virginia read to her a lot during the time Margaret was getting better.

Roe had an Overland car. One evening they double-dated to a movie. It was a beautiful moonlit night. After the movie, the four decided to drive to Springfield, nine miles away. The roads back then were mostly ground rock and were called pikes, not roads. About a mile out of Springfield the car lights went out. Roe and Bill could not get them to work, so they drove very slowly in to Springfield. It was rather late, and all the garages were closed, as they usually "rolled up the streets" at nine o'clock. They ended up having to drive back to Lebanon by moonlight which took a long time. They did not get home until very late, and Margaret recalled getting a chewing-out by Lillian. She informed Margaret, "I don't care if you were with the minister's son!" Lillian never really worried all that much, though, as she always told Roe when they left on a date, "Now, Roe, I am depending on you taking good care of my little girl." Roe was several years older than Margaret and was always a perfect gentleman.

The next two years Margaret was attending Logan College at Russellville, Kentucky. It was a Methodist college for girls that opened around the time of the Civil War, about 1861, and closed its doors in the early '30s, most likely as a result of the great depression. She played on the college basketball team, taught swimming and diving, and often took over the gym class for the teacher. She won her letter in both basketball and swimming, but perhaps excelled the most in dramatics which was her best subject. They called it elocution or expression in those days. She took part in many plays, including

Shakespeare, and the theatre remained one of her greatest interests in future life.

Courting, Career and Future

Much of Margaret and Roe's courting ended up being done by letter or by telephone. Roe still had not found exactly what he wanted to do with his life. During the time of uncertainty, he went on the Chautauqua circuit as a music director and in charge of young people. Following that he was District Attorney for a while but really did not like that role, and finally went to Kansas City in 1922 as music director in charge of the youth group, as well as conducting the Wednesday night services at the First Presbyterian Church. One of his choir members was Marian Talley.

It was at this time he became very interested in the Boy Scouting program. He had a Boy Scout troop and could see the marvelous opportunity to mold young lives from age 12 to 21, and develop responsible citizens of the future equal to the future. He was seeking the right career path all this time, and he was approached with a job offer from the Boy Scouts of America. He had practiced law long enough to know he really did not want to spend his life in the courts. It rubbed him the wrong way to have to plea clients innocent when he himself felt the person guilty. During his entire life, his knowledge of the law would always be advantageous to him, but it did not take Roe long to make up his mind about the job offer. He accepted the position of Boy Scout Executive of the state of Wyoming. In January 1923 he attended the Boy Scout training sessions. He bid his parents and Margaret goodbye and headed for Wyoming.

Wyoming brought out "the cowboy" in the new scout executive.

Promises and Dreams

We are now at the point where Roe has asked Margaret to marry him, and she had informed him until he made up his mind what he wanted to do with his life and had a steady job, she would not consider marriage. In Roe's mind he had settled on his life's work and was in Casper, Wyoming, as the Scout Executive of this small but widespread council covering the entire state of Wyoming. He was enthusiastic about every aspect of his new position. He loved it and had truly found what he wanted to do with his life. It was a marvelous challenge, and he was ready to tackle everything and anything that would result in achieving his goals of an effective program that would attract youth. His main worry was that Margaret would not wait for him.

By now Roe had been in Casper, Wyoming, for a year.

That was certainly time enough to ensure Margaret he had made his career decision. She had promised him when he had finally settled down and knew what he wanted to do with his life that she would marry him. They were married on September 26, 1923.

On that date, the happy couple was in St. Joseph, Missouri, to be married by Roe's dad who had become the minister of the Second Presbyterian Church. They both wanted to be married by Roe's dad, but it was a disappointment to Margaret that she could not be married in Kentucky where all her friends could have been in attendance. The only people present on her side of the family were her aunt and uncle. It is my understanding that she got married in gray velvet, not of her choosing, and there were never any pictures of the bride and groom. There is one picture of the church lavishly decorated. Margaret was on "Cloud Nine" that she was marrying Roe, but sad that none of her friends could be present.

It is interesting how their lives went in a circle. They spent their honeymoon in Kansas City, Missouri, and while in Kansas City, Margaret had the opportunity of meeting many of Roe's friends, some of whom became important in their later lives.

The city was not new to Margaret, as she had been there to visit her Aunt Ola in the past, another sister of her father. Ola's husband was a contractor who built many of the homes around 43rd to 45th and Holly to Jarboe Street and from 57th to 59th Streets just west of Brookside up to Wornall Road. The streets were all mud at that time, she recollected. As a child, she and her cousin Cecil toured the Unideda Biscuit Company along with the rest of the family. Receiving crackers and cookies had been a delight, but the chocolate-covered marshmallow ones were the best!

Back to the honeymoon, it was a long way west and north to Casper, Wyoming. The roads were not paved, and 25 to 30 miles an hour was as fast as one could travel. The further north they went, the colder it got. Margaret's teeth were chattering by the time they arrived in Casper, as there were no heaters in cars at that time.

This was in the Salt Pot Dome days. The town was wide open, and yet you could go any place and be safe. They started their married life in an apartment. Roe had taken his meals in boarding houses and hotels for such a long time that he was looking forward to home-cooked meals, and insisted on having waffles every morning swimming in butter and syrup. The young couple did not have an electric waffle iron, so Margaret had to use iron ones that cooked on top of the stove. The waffles always smoked so much that Margaret was sure all the other people in the building were delighted when they moved to a house.

Roe weighed 190 pounds when they were married and was 6 feet, 4 inches tall. He put on 100 pounds the first year of marriage. Actually, he taught Margaret how to cook for, according to him, all she could do was boil water! He went home for lunch nearly every day, and wanted a good-sized meal at noon. For the evening meal he always insisted on meat, potatoes, gravy, salad, biscuit or bread and, of course, dessert. Margaret always fixed everything that Roe wanted as she wanted to please him. She did, however, at times try to persuade him he did not really need to eat four or five pieces of bread piled high with butter with his meals, that he really did not need bread at all, but Roe always won that argument, and bread remained on the menu.

The weather seemed more severe back in the '20s, at least it was in Wyoming. Roe had been up in Riverton at the Indian reservation and arrived home late one night with his feet nearly frozen. He felt he might never walk again. Margaret put his feet in cold water and gradually added hot to it in order to thaw his feet. His feet bothered him the rest of his life, but he tried not to let that ever be visible to anyone else.

Roe spent at least a day a week over in Riverton at the Wind River Indian reservation. He had several scout troops on the reservation and had become friends with Chief Lone Bear of the Arapaho tribe. Lone Bear was very old at the time. Roe loved the hours he spent talking with the chief, and as time went on, he learned everything he could from him regarding the history of his people, their beliefs, thoughts, traditions and way of life. All of this fascinated Roe Bartle. He explained to the old chief the dreams he had of instilling in youth through the Scouting program the wonderful things he had learned from him. He saw all these things as character-building factors that would provide an important dimension to Scouting. The chief also told him there were physical and mental tests that all the young members of the tribe had to go through before they could become braves.

Before leaving Casper, Chief Lone Bear made Roe a blood brother. He was taken into the tribe, and the old chief gave Roe his own name, which was an honor Roe humbly accepted. All this information got his brain cells percolating with ideas of how he could enrich the program of Boy Scouting. He mulled over all he had learned until he arrived in St. Joseph, Missouri, where he was able to translate the teachings into reality. Chief Lone Bear of

Riverton died soon after Roe moved to Missouri.

With his characteristic tireless energy, Roe taught a large Sunday School class each week. It was a men's Bible class with professional men, bankers, doctors, insurance men, etc. Consequently, Roe and Margaret could never go out on a Saturday night as that was when Roe prepared his lesson. He would work on it from dinner to midnight, or after. The lessons were so popular, he soon found men coming from other faiths and great distances to join his class.

In that nearly every night Roe was busy with some kind of Scout meeting, to keep herself occupied Margaret did a lot of sewing, letter writing and reading. In addition, she got involved in a couple of plays. The rehearsals were at night, and one evening she blacked out and scared the cast and director. It was so warm on the stage that she just passed out. When they brought her back around, she informed one and all that she was pregnant. The director, Cora, and her husband, Everet, were good friends of Margaret and Roe, and when hearing Margaret's statement, Cora said she had news for Margaret. She, too, was pregnant with her second child. When the play was over and they had time to discuss personal matters, they found they were due about the same time. The two of them spent months making baby clothes and tried to walk about five miles a day.

That summer Roe was going to be at the Scout camp all summer. He did not want Margaret to be alone, therefore sent her to Kentucky to visit her family and friends. She had a full, busy summer in Danville, Lebanon and Lexington. Her younger sister, Ruth, returned to Casper with Margaret and planned to stay on until after the baby was born.

The month was November, and it was 40 degrees below zero. It was so cold they had to put coal oil in the water to keep it from freezing. Margaret woke Roe up at three-thirty in the morning for the trip to the hospital. Dr. Harvey had a small private hospital which his patients preferred. It was a mighty cold drive to the hospital. Roe drove carefully on the icy snow, while Margaret reassured him they would arrive in plenty of time. At nine-fifteen in the morning Margaret gave birth to a baby girl. The date was November 27, 1924, which was Thanksgiving Day. Instead of a turkey, the front page of the Casper paper told of the stork arriving at Chief Bartle's household.

After much deliberation, the wee lassie was named Margaret Mae. Explanation being: One grandmother was Margaret Mae, the other Ada Mae, the aunt that raised Margaret was Lillian Mae, and Margaret's youngest sister was Anna Mae. At the age of 12, this newest Margaret Mae legally changed her name to Margaret Roe which she felt it should have been in the first place. She hated the name Mae with a passion.

Friend Cora entered the hospital two days later and was delivered of her second son, John. In those days new mothers were kept in the hospital for 10 days to two weeks. Cora and Margaret looked forward to the evenings when Everet and Roe would come for their visits. Miss Reipy, the nurse, would push the girls' beds together, making it easier for them to play bridge with the fellows, and usually an hour or so later she would show up with refreshments for the four of them. When the time came for the new fathers to leave, she would usher them to the door, telling them the new mommies needed their rest.

Soon after the proud dad brought his family home, he informed Margaret they would be moving to St.

Joseph, Missouri. Margaret was rather upset as she had learned to love Casper despite the cold and had made many friends. Roe had taken her with him nearly everywhere, except when she had gone to Kentucky for the summer. She knew practically everyone in Casper.

Margaret's last sweet memory of Casper was the afternoon Roe arrived on the scene with a small Christmas tree. He insisted on decorating it himself. Margaret was not able to do too much, as most of her energy was consumed in taking care of the baby and packing everything up for the move. Her sister Ruth did the cooking, laundry and other household chores so Margaret would be free to do the other things. When Roe finished decorating the tree and had the lights on, he took his daughter out to the tree and told her all about Christmas, baby Jesus, and sang softly to her, "Silent Night." Although she was only a little over three weeks old, Roe had her complete attention. Margaret always treasured this as a sweet and loving memory of their days in Casper, Wyoming.

A Bartle family gathering in St. Joseph, Missouri — Sam — Margaret — Ada — and Jimmy standing between her grandparents — summer of 1926.

Pony Express

As the train from Casper approached the station in St. Joseph, January 1925, the welcoming committee was on hand to greet their new Boy Scout Executive and his family. Roe, Margaret and their wee daughter were delighted with their warm welcome. Upon their arrival, Margaret handed her baby daughter, who was in a basket, to a young Boy Scout named Don Baldwin. When Margaret Mae was just five weeks of age, Don Baldwin became her first baby sitter, and continued to be such for some time to come. Much to the families' delight there was a period when Don lived with the Bartles, and Roe became a definite role model who greatly influenced the future course of Don's life.

Margaret, with the help of her sister Ruth, got nicely settled in the new home Roe had secured for the family before they moved to St. Joseph. Moving to St. Joseph, of course, brought about a reunion with Roe's parents, Ada and Sam. Margaret had a dinner for them on the evening Margaret Mae reached the age of five weeks. It was good for Roe to be back with his parents and tried to spend as much time as possible with them, as they were marvelous counselors for him, as well as great supporters of what he was trying to formulate and accomplish.

Roe was delighted with his new challenge. He had an ideal board — one that was open to suggestions and change, as well as monetary and voluntary leadership support. One of the board members, actually the president of the board, Wiley O. Cox, became a cherished friend and was Margaret Mae's godfather. His large, beautifully appointed home was always open for meetings and friends. Much warmth and cordiality was felt within those walls.

At last Roe was going to be able to launch his plans for the Tribe of Mic-O-Say at summer camp. This would be a first in any Boy Scout Council. When Roe arrived in St. Joseph, there had been only 62 Boy Scouts attending summer camp. He was confident that commencement of Mic-O-Say which would honor outstanding Scouts would not only bring more boys to camp, but would also increase Scouting membership. On May 23-24, 1925, he began his Tribe of Mic-O-Say, awarding 11 eagle claws. Due to being Council president, Wiley O. Cox was given the first claw and became the second member of Mic-O-Say. In time Wiley became affectionately known to all as "Dad" Cox, and he became the first man to receive the Silver Antelope Award in the Council.

Most likely, due to the interest generated in Mic-O-Say, 196 boys attended the first session at Camp Brinton in 1925. In those early days there was no tapping ceremony. Braves wore a single claw while Warriors wore two claws. A down-turned double claw identified an honorary member. Roe made all of the decisions as to who would be inducted. He was Chief and conducted all the ceremonies.

By 1926 there were 40 troops with 741 Boy Scouts in the Council, and Camp Brinton was listed as a Grade A camp. Three hundred and five boys, almost one-half of the membership, attended camp that summer. Wiley O. Cox was named as the first honorary Chieftain. It was also during this year that several boys had the privilege of attending a special camp in Noel, Missouri, and the outstanding Boy Scout for St. Joseph was chosen. He was Boyce Brandon and, as a result of his selection, won a trip to Hot Springs, Arkansas, where he attended the national conference of Scout officials. Roe accompanied the young man to this conference. While there, Boyce was selected to be in an honor troop of 32 Boy Scouts under the leadership of Dan Beard, the National Boy Scout Commissioner. A long-term friendship between Roe and Dan Beard started at this time.

In November of that year, Will Rogers dropped in on the Regional Boy Scout Executive board meeting. He kept everyone laughing throughout the dinner hour with his talk.

March 16, 1927, Roe organized Troop KFEQ, the first radio Lone Scout troop in the world. This opened up more new worlds to these young men living in remote areas where Scout troops were not available. Broadcasts were made each Sunday evening at 7:15. The Boy Scout oath was broadcast across the airwaves when new members joined the troop, and people throughout the land became more familiar with Scouting and its principles.

Roe was always organizing something new and doing projects that made for good and interesting articles for the newspapers. As a result of his news reporting experience in Chattanooga, Roe made sure that articles were written for the *St. Joseph Gazette* and *News Press* telling the citizens of St. Joseph all about the program and future planning of their Boy Scout Council. He even supervised a street clean-up for St. Joseph, and three of the Scout participants were awarded a free week at Camp Brinton that summer.

Under Roe's guidance the Council had expanded their area to 17 counties including northwest Missouri and northeast Kansas. By the summer of 1927 new buildings and facilities were added at Camp Brinton due to the number of Boy Scouts attending summer camp. There were 1,203 boys in 58 active troops and, as a result, a fall membership drive grew to 1,406 by year's end.

In August of 1927 Roe organized a covered wagon trek involving two patrols from St. Joseph. The Scouts made their way to nearly every town and village in northwest Missouri and northeast Kansas. They were received everywhere with great interest, and once again this made marvelous publicity for the Boy Scout organization. Part of their entertainment for the public were Indian dances the boys performed in Indian costume attire around the campfire.

It was at this time because of the phenomenal growth of Scouting in St. Joseph that Roe was invited to Chicago to explain his program and method. After completing the conference, there was unanimous approval of the 630 laymen representing 106 councils to adopt his program, and it became known as the "St. Joseph Plan."

Roe traveled throughout the area of his Council to establish new troops and to deliver talks on his program for youth. Speaking in churches, his topic was "The Church's Part in the American Boy Problem." He spoke at Masonic Temples, Rotary Clubs and many clubs and other organizations whenever he had the opportunity to tell most people about the program of Scouting. The Boy Scout Jamboree gave family members, as well as the public at large, a glimpse of Boy Scout activities and the excitement of the Mic-O-Say Indian dancers in their colorful regalia. All the talks and appearances made for favorable newsprint, and in his way Roe kept Boy Scouting in the public eye. During the summer months of camping, articles regarding activities at Camp Brinton found their way into the newspapers several times each week.

On July 21, 1928, it was noted that Roe was not in camp, but had made a trip "on business" to Kansas City, Missouri. He was very interested in the Kansas City, Missouri Council for the Scout Executive position which he would accept later on in the year.

In the meantime during the month of September, the local Boy Scout office received word that Roe had been elected as one of 12 National Executive Board Members. The local Boy Scout community beamed with pride with the recognition of its young executive who had made such tremendous strides in the previous four years and who had focused national attention on the Scouting movement in St. Joseph.

October 3, 1928, Roe informed his St. Joseph board he was resigning, effective January 1, 1929, as he had accepted the position of Scout Executive and would be moving to Kansas City, Missouri. Roe told them, "It is with genuine regret that I am leaving St. Joseph. One could not ask for a better home and business surroundings than we have found here. I came here as a stranger four years ago, and in a comparatively short time I was surrounded by friends. The advancement of Boy Scouting in St. Joseph has been unusual, but the credit reverts to the men who have divided their time between business and providing leadership in the community. I feel I will have an opportunity to add further strength and growth to Scouting by moving to Kansas City. Then, too, it is the wish of the national organization that I take up this new challenge."

The St. Joseph chapter was closing in many ways other than just Scouting. Roe had kept himself available, concentrating his energy with as many people as possible. As a result he had become an active and participating member of Kiwanis, the Metropolitan Club, Booster Clubs, the Chamber of Commerce, the Ministerial Alliance, the American Legion, and served as president of the local lodge of Eagles.

To sum up Roe's four years in St. Joseph, he increased the Boy Scout membership from 420 Boy Scouts to 1,785. He began the Jamboree, camporee and Scoutmaster training, as well as courses in Scoutcraft at the junior college. He organized the first black troop in the area, once again ahead of the times in many, many ways. Summer camp attendance increased from 62 in 1925 to 584 in 1928. Mic-O-Say flourished and helped stimulate Boy Scouts to higher achievement throughout the winter months, working toward attending another summer at camp in hopes that one day they, too, would be called to the tribe.

Many years later in a letter to Simon Rozitsky, Roe wrote of his St. Joseph venture, "We were doing so many things that were unorthodox but still basic Boy Scouting, and it was just hard for them to believe that such could be possible. The 100 percent teamwork that this old man had from the wonderful volunteers and the crazy ideas that were created in his mind in the days of his youthful Executiveship certainly put me in high places professionally. I realize that I was an illegitimate Scout Executive, and I was an outlaw Scout Executive — that I was an unpredictable Scout Executive as well as a professional leading of Scouting who should have been shot at sunrise on many occasions as the years passed. My God — it has been a lot of fun."

He was moving on … At this time, St. Joseph ranked 62nd, while the Kansas City Council was the 14th largest council in the country.

On December 9, 1928, the Boy Scouts of south St. Joseph held the first farewell event for Roe, and on the 12th a grand farewell banquet was held at the Robidoux Hotel. It was reported to be the largest Scout social event ever held in the city. Margaret and Roe were given a gladstone bag and a silver tea service. December 26th Roe spent the day straightening up his office, and his last day in the St. Joseph office was December 28, 1928.

In our St. Joseph Scouting family I personally remember, besides Dad Cox, are Simon Rozitsky, Finley Fiske, Joseph Scanlon, and Eben S. Thresher who came to St. Joseph from Kansas City to be the camp waterfront director in 1928. I must add, they all remained a great part of the lives of the Bartle Clan throughout the many years that followed.

Now that we know how Roe spent a greater part of his

time, let us not forget Margaret and the Bartle family life. The first year Margaret was busy with Margaret Mae, plus making clothes for her, visiting with Ada and Sam, having them over for dinner a lot, and attending church, sewing circles, and in all was busy making new friends.

Margaret and Roe enjoyed playing cards, especially pinochle, pitch and bridge. Dominoes and other games were played as well and always made for a relaxing evening. A favorite card-playing fun couple were Rita and Wendell Urquhart, who had a son several years older than Margaret Mae. Margaret always looked forward to getting together with them as they would usually plan on having dinner together before playing cards, and she knew Roe would let down, relax and forget about meetings, committees and future challenges for a short while anyway. Both did as much church-related work as time would permit and, of course, attended regularly, though Roe did not make it every Sunday, as he was often called to speak at other churches. Margaret and the baby were there each week, and during the church service, when Margaret Mae was a baby, she was placed in a basket behind the organ where she usually slept until the services were over.

Another family entered their lives at this time and became lifelong friends. They were Evelyn and Byron Hunt. They had two sons, Robert, four years older than Margaret Mae, and Joseph, who was two years older. As time went on, the boys used to ask their mother, "Why does that girl always have to tag along?" Evelyn was not only a very close friend but was always a source of help and advice in the areas of cooking, sewing and general planning. Margaret loved her like a sister. Byron was an officer of a St. Joseph bank and had met Roe through the church and his interest in Scouting. They became close friends, greatly respected each other and shared many ideals and interests. It was a friendship that would change the path of Byron Hunt's life.

When Margaret Mae was 18 months old, Margaret made a trip back to Kentucky to introduce and show her off to her family and friends. It was wonderful to get back and see everyone and catch up on all the news and gossip. Margaret Mae, although her schedule had been completely upset as she and mother were constantly on the go, was a good baby and, of course, thoroughly loved all the attention.

During the winter of 1927, when Margaret Mae was three years old, she contracted double pneumonia and was very seriously ill. The doctor came by the house each morning and evening to check on her and insisted that Margaret give her a liquid medicine twice a day. Margaret tried in every way to get Margaret Mae to swallow the medicine — but to no avail. She got so upset she called Roe crying and telling him her tale of woe. He came home to prove to her that there was nothing to it — but once again the child won. When the doctor came that evening, they informed him of their dilemma. The doctor proceeded to show them how to complete the mission. When he turned around to tell them, "See, there is nothing to it," it was at this point that Margaret Mae blew the whole mouthful of medicine all over her bed and the doctor. Nonetheless, she recovered despite her naughty ways and the lack of medical benefits.

That summer, Margaret and her daughter went camping down on the Little Blue River. Margaret was always a very strong and beautiful swimmer. She wanted to swim way down the river and asked some of the ladies if they would please keep an eye on Margaret Mae until she returned. They complied and watched her swim away. When the ladies turned around, the child was nowhere to be seen. They really panicked and all rushed toward the shore to start the search. One of the ladies stumbled over something and reached down to see what it was — only to discover it was the child. Margaret Mae had walked out into the water trying to catch her little sailboat and, missing it, she sat on the bottom and played with the pretty rocks until she passed out. The lady grabbed her up, and they rolled her on a barrel to remove all the water in her lungs and revive her. Much to their relief, their efforts were successful and Margaret Mae was none the worse for her adventure. Fearing she might have a relapse, the ladies informed Margaret of their horrifying experience while she was gone. Margaret knew then, the next project was to teach her daughter to swim, which actually took several years to accomplish.

Roe arrived home one afternoon just in time to see Margaret Mae go speeding down the basement steps on her kiddie car. Figuring she had bounced into the basement wall and was probably badly hurt, he took about two steps to make it down the flight of steps, only to find her looking up and giggling at him. Nonetheless, this little episode shook Roe up, and Margaret was thankful he was home at that time. They both agreed this little daughter of theirs was a handful, quite a challenge and lucky to be alive.

As the time drew near for Margaret and Roe to bid farewell to all their friends in St. Joseph, Margaret got a feeling of loneliness. She again had made many lovely friends, and once again she was moving and would be missing contact with them. It did give her some comfort that she had made some friends when she and Roe had been in Kansas City five years previously, and hopefully they would return to St. Joseph from time to time and renew their friendships. Once again she packed up and made ready for their move. They were honored by friends and Scouting acquaintances, sending them off with wonderful and endearing memories of their St. Joseph venture.

Margaret Roe Bartle — four years old
playing on the Blue River

The new Boy Scout executive for Kansas City, Missouri — 1929

Heart of America

Another very different New Year's Eve and New Year's Day for the Bartle family. Upon their arrival in Kansas City they went to the Senate Hotel at Armour and Campbell, as this was to be their home for the following months. They wanted to get their bearings in this large city before making a decision on a permanent residence. Unpacking all the storage boxes and getting all their possessions put away kept Margaret busy, while Roe was getting his desk at the office in order and setting up his agenda for the first week as Boy Scout Executive of the Kansas City Area Council.

Roe was more than busy that first year trying to get his program of Scouting in the works... board meetings, committee meetings, speeches to deliver, professional staff to hire as well as office workers. He worked long and full hours, and more times than Margaret liked he would work a seven-day week. This left Margaret with a lot of free time to fill and many hours of loneliness.

Margaret Mae was enrolled in Barstow School for Girls where she attended kindergarten each day. Riding the bus to and from was great fun. She enjoyed meeting and making new friends, plus learning new games, having interesting stories read to the class, and other activities. The only thing she disliked at the school was the outfit she had to wear for gym. It consisted of bloomers and a white shirt that buttoned down the front and at the crotch. Nonetheless, it was a very interesting year with many new experiences for her.

Wanting to keep herself busy and desiring to make her free time worthwhile, unbeknown to Roe, Margaret enrolled in the Cleveland Chiropractic College. Being located close to the hotel made it convenient for Margaret to walk back and forth. She enjoyed her studies, and it filled her empty hours. She was looking forward to becoming Dr. Bartle. How Roe found out about her latest endeavor is a mystery — but he did, and there was quite an argument which ended with Margaret quitting the college. There would be only one bread winner in the Bartle family, and that would be Roe — end of discussion.

Roe dearly loved Margaret's long flowing hair. When out in public, she wore it in a bun at the nape of her neck. She disliked all this hair. Being naturally curly as well as long, it was a chore to wash and dry, and she felt her appearance was that of an old woman. One afternoon she got brave, went to the beauty/barber shop and told the operator to cut it like the latest "flapper" style. Never being definitely coiffed in the latest style, she felt very glamorous and was thrilled with her new look. She had

Roe's favorite dinner ready that evening with candlelight and all the trimmings. The evening was a complete fiasco. Roe was more than furious. After he informed her of his strong feelings about the whole situation, he said little else to her for nearly a week. Later on, Margaret felt he must have noticed that most of the women in Kansas City were "up to date" wearing the short, short hair style. He apologized to Margaret about his big blow-up over the matter.

To get a little exercise, fresh air and to give Margaret Mae an outing, Margaret would take her for long walks, often ending up around 31st and Troost which was lined with stores of all kinds. They had a lot of fun window shopping, and it helped educate her daughter in many ways, regarding people, merchandise, money, and how to act around strangers and in other situations.

When Roe arrived as Boy Scout Executive of the Kansas City Area Council, the summer camp was located at Noel, Missouri. It was Camp Sayre, named after the man who had given the property. The younger Scouts enjoyed the camp, but the older boys needed a place providing more challenges. During the 1929 summer session at Camp Sayre, the Tribe of Mic-O-Say began with the call of many foxmen who started their long trail to the inner circle. Those that I personally remember were L.G. Soule, W.M. Grube, Cliff Tozier, Joe Harbaugh, Fred Coldwell, Howard Kroh, Jr. and Keith Oehschlager.

The camp was not big enough to camp all the boys of the growing council. The search for a new and adequate site began. Roe and Ernie Modlin, the staff member for camping, kept busy looking for property — acreage that would provide a worthwhile site. Ernie Modlin was the one who found what he felt to be ideal.

After inspecting it, the Camping Committee recommended 460 acres be purchased. This acreage makes up the present Camp Wigwam portion of the Roe Bartle Reservation. It was purchased in the fall of 1929. Clearing began immediately, and the camp was named Camp Osceola after the small town nearby. On July 7, 1930, began the first of four two-week sessions for that summer. The cost was $16 for a two-week session, and the boys arrived by train from Kansas City to Osceola and then were trucked to camp from there. Ernie Modlin became the first camp director.

The campers watched the stars at night from the point and swam in the Osage River during the day. Two permanent buildings were installed that first year, one being a small log cabin which was the camp director's quarters, and the Nature Lodge, a two-story structure. Both buildings remain and are used in camp today. The dining hall was a large tent in the middle of camp. The Tribe of Mic-O-Say became a focal point of camp tradition and activity. The younger boys were in awe of the Scouts who proudly wore their eagle claws. It gave them a desire to work harder to return to camp, and always have the hope that some day they, too, would be called to the Tribe. The Tribal Council for some time consisted of Ernie Modlin as the principal Medicine Man ... the others were "Pappy" or Pop" Grube, "Doc" Soule and Don Baldwin, and Roe, of course, was Chief. In 1935 Don Baldwin became the second camp director, and the Chief named him "Skipper."

It should be added at this point that it was during the first year at Osceola that Roe introduced his daughter as his "one and only Jimmy." During the summer months, Jimmy had a boy's haircut and wore boy's clothes; therefore many thought she was a boy! I might add, due to this, during WWII there were many who asked Roe if his Jimmy was in the Atlantic or Pacific — at which time he had to inform them that Jimmy was a girl, thus she was doing her part in the war effort on the homefront through working for the Red Cross, Canteen and U.S.O.

In the big city, another move was made to make life easier and more convenient for the whole family. The family moved from the Senate Hotel to the Casa Loma East. It was the first apartment building in a long string of apartments on the south side of Brush Creek between Main Street and Wornall Road. More new friends were made, as the apartments were filled with many children. Life there was not dull, and there was never a problem about children being cared for at any time of the day or night. Margaret Mae, whom we will refer to from here on out as Jimmy, attended first and second grade at E.C. White Grade School, which was located on the corner of Main and Brookside just one block from the apartment.

Jimmy had never been around dogs and knew nothing about them. One afternoon a neighbor lady invited her over for some warm, freshly baked cookies. When she entered the door, there was this barking toy terrier which scared her so badly that she ran to the piano bench, climbed up on it, and then ended up standing on top of the upright piano. Margaret, as well as the neighbor lady, could not believe this tiny dog could put the child into such amazing action. They had a good laugh out of it. Jimmy did not get down until the dog was locked in the bedroom, but the delicious cookies helped her forget this horrible experience.

Being on the Plaza was a joy for Margaret and her daughter. The convenience of everything meant a great deal, as they had no car. Roe drove their only car and, of course, needed it throughout the day. The streetcar, however, got them wherever they wished, whether it might be downtown, over to 31st and Troost again, or out to Waldo and the Country Club area of the city.

The day Roe brought home exciting news for Margaret was when he informed her he had talked Byron Hunt, of St. Joseph, Missouri, into leaving the banking business and joining his staff at the Boy Scout office. This delighted both of them, and it was a great day when Byron and Evelyn arrived in Kansas City. The first home remembered by Jimmy was at 6434 Wornall Road, and again she had her "Ma Hunt" to stay with and the boys to "bug" once again. Byron, "Pa Hunt," felt he would be most effective in the office and not as a camp staffer. This had been agreed with Roe, and he stuck by it, and Byron only went to camp as a visitor or for special reasons. At the same time, Roe felt good knowing Byron was in the office keeping on top of things while Roe was at camp. Both Hunt boys, Bob, known as "Salty," and Joe, known as "Kinky," were in camp each summer. Therefore Ma Hunt brought her dog Corky and would visit Margaret at the ranch for several weeks during the summer.

Margaret and Roe joined Central Presbyterian Church at Armour and Campbell, February 1929, while living at the Senate Hotel. It might be noted that their membership was never moved to another church, and they were faithful members, both becoming elders, and Roe was Clerk of the Session. He was also on several national Presbyterian boards in Atlanta, Georgia, and Richmond, Virginia. Both Margaret and Roe loved their church wholeheartedly. Wednesday night family dinners were held each week in the church and were always scheduled for Margaret and Jimmy, as Roe would be attending meetings, making a speech or working late at the office.

As the '30s rolled in, besides many changes at camp, there were changes on the homefront as the family moved first to East 68th Street near Oak Street, then to 3 East 69th Street, and finally 19 East 70th Street. Later, in the '40s, they purchased a house at 25 East 70th Street, which was their home until a few years after Jimmy got married. They then sold their home and moved to the Plaza House Apartments, 4712 Roanoke Parkway, where they lived until each passed away.

During the summers of 1928 through 1931, the senior Bartles wanted to have Margaret Mae visit them. She became quite a traveler, starting at the age of four when Margaret and Roe would put her on the train to Little Rock, Arkansas, where she would transfer to another train for Fordyce, Arkansas, where Sam was now the minister of the Presbyterian Church. Roe would generously tip the conductor and the porter, with instructions to look after his daughter until she arrived at her destination. This was repeated four summers in a row, and Jimmy was treated like a princess all the way. She had a lot of fun. On one trip, after eating her dinner, she was too full to eat the watermelon dessert. The waiter told her to come back later; he would be happy to hold it for her, and that she did. She loved riding the train, seeing all the sights along the way, and from all reports was always quite a little lady.

When the move was made to 68th Street, Jimmy completed her grade school education at J.C. Nichols Grade School located at 69th and Oak. She was able to walk to school, home for lunch, back to school, and home again each day. It was while living in this house that Roe planned a surprise anniversary party for Margaret. Margaret had been painting all day and had on her old paint pants and shirt. Jimmy, knowing of the party, tried to get her mother to bathe and dress before dinner. Thinking it would be just a warm-up dinner for her and Jimmy, she refused to do as requested. Before long Roe popped in and asked Margaret to go for a ride with him to run an errand. She complied, and while they were gone, all the guests arrived. When they returned, Margaret wondered why the house was so dark, but figured Jimmy had gone to bed. It was truly a complete surprise when she walked in, and the lights were turned on. She gave Jimmy a very dirty look as if to say, "Why did you not warn me?" as there she stood in her paint clothes, no make-up, and her hair a mess. She excused herself immediately, ran upstairs and made herself presentable. Needless to say, she had a wonderful time, and what started out on a bad note turned into a lively evening of fun and good fellowship. She and Jimmy laughed about the "big secret" the next day. Roe was proud of Jimmy for keeping such a secret from her mother.

Bartle Ranch

Roe did not want to leave his family in the city all summer while he was in camp. So it was much to his delight that he was able to purchase a ranch, 5,000 acres plus, where Margaret and Jimmy could spend their summers. The ranch was only 10 miles from the Scout camp. The main house was built by an Indian. It was unique, as it was a log cabin made with the bark left on the logs which were perpendicular, and chinked between each log. The stone fireplace was large enough to hold logs from a whole tree in the wintertime, and a fun place for Jimmy to play house in during the summertime. The house was not fancy, but it had all the room that was necessary. Two huge bedrooms at each end, a long wide room in the middle that was the dining room on one end, and the living room on the other end, where on the wall above the upright piano was a huge buffalo head. There was a small bathroom and a kitchen with a wood-burning stove, as well as a kerosene one. The ice box was large enough to stand up in, and it held 1,000 pounds of ice. A few feet away from the back porch was another building which housed the couple who did the cooking and cleaning for the summer months. Attached behind their quarters was a bunk house consisting of five rooms. There were two sets of bunk beds in each room, so when out-of-town guests came there was always plenty of room for all to sleep. There was also a "two-holer," down the path out back, which always had Sears or Wards catalogues to read!

The minute school was out, Margaret and Jimmy packed up and left for Osceola and the ranch. This was an ideal setting for Jimmy's summers. Margaret spent the summer reading all the magazines she had received in the past nine months, getting letters answered, horseback riding and swimming. There was a spring-fed creek that was great to swim in, as long as one watched out for snakes and leeches. Cattle, sheep, hogs, chickens and horses were on the ranch, and all the feed was raised, as well as vegetables. Jimmy had fun down through the years milking cows, mowing hay, pitching it on the hay wagon, and getting the horse-drawn wagon to the barn to pitch the hay in the loft. She cut corn, gathered eggs and vegetables. She helped to break horses and spent many a

"Thibby" keeping Roe company while relaxing at the ranch.

day riding her horse from sun up until sundown. A favorite hobby was hunting snakes, boiling them, making things out of their skin, bleaching their vertebra, and making jewelry out of them, adding small arrowheads found in the fields and pastures. One such memory: Jimmy had found a variety of about 10 large snakes which she placed in a huge bucket. She boiled these on a campfire down by the creek. She was called to lunch, tried to ignore the call, but in time had to rush up to the house, swallow lunch whole, and dashed back to the creek where she found the hogs had located her prize batch and decided it would make a nice lunch for them. Jimmy was heartbroken as her snake hunt had been tedious, and now there was nothing left but an empty bucket and a few coals from the fire.

Another incident with the snakes at the ranch occurred when Roe came over for lunch one day. Jimmy met him at the main gate with a colorful milk snake contained in one of his cigar boxes. She rode in the car with him to the house and left the cigar box in the car with the lid nailed shut. After lunch, she went out to get the box, only to find that it was empty, as the snake had forced itself out of the box and completely disappeared. Jimmy never told Roe of the escape, and the snake never showed up again — another lost treasure ... just as well this time!

Margaret rode the prize horse on the ranch. His name was "Black Beauty" and that he was... a very spirited and gorgeous piece of horse flesh. Her favorite time to ride was at night by moonlight. There were always enough horses at the ranch for family and friends, plus 50 or 60 which were loaned to Scout Camp each summer. C.F. "Key" Cole was in charge of equitation. Many Scouts were able to pass their horsemanship merit badge while at camp, something they would never be able to do in the city. During the winter months Roe would lend horses to surrounding farmers for their children to ride to school, as it was much too far to walk, and cars for many years were not to be had by these Ozark folk.

Kerosene and propane lamps were used in the early days at the ranch. Later Roe had a generator house built with batteries all around the ledge. If the generator pumped all day long to sufficiently charge the batteries, there was electricity available each evening and, if not, it was back to the lamps again. Ceiling fans were installed, which were a great help during the hot, hot summers when it would be nearly 110 and no breeze.

One summer when Roe was back up in the city for a few days he had learned that heavy rain storms were falling at camp. He felt he had to get hold of Margaret at the ranch to make sure the family was okay. The phone at the ranch house happened to be on the bathroom wall. It was an antique crank wall phone, and the telephone operator in Osceola would ring us up. That she did. Margaret came to the phone, and while talking she leaned on the basin. The next thing Jimmy knew, her mother was yelling from the bathtub. It seems that lightning had struck close by, and she had been pitched into the tub. Jimmy grabbed the phone and told Roe all was well, but they were not going to talk on the phone any more until the storm was over. From that time on, Margaret would seldom use that phone when there was a storm.

When Scout officials and their wives came to visit the camp and ranch, the men stayed at camp and the women would stay at the ranch, as Roe always felt the only women in camp should be the nurses and cooks. Margaret and Jimmy always loved having company, but when their guests were from New York or New Jersey, they really got a big kick out of them, as they would always inquire about where were the Indians, were we ever bothered much by them, and was it safe to be there? It seemed unbelievable that people still thought we had such problems west of the Mississippi. All the questions and disbeliefs made for a different kind of summer entertainment for Jimmy. Outside games that occupied everyone were horseshoes, archery and croquet.

Jimmy had to find fun and entertainment for herself. Therefore she made friends with the children of the men who lived and worked on the ranch. Her best times were spent with Claude and Vergie Mulkey. When they were first married, they spent their honeymoon in a small cabin just inside the main gate. After working for Roe for several years, however, Claude became the foreman of the ranch, and they moved to the large house down by the barn. While Margaret napped in the afternoons, Jimmy could be found down in the cabin with Vergie. They could be sewing, cooking, canning, making craft items, playing cards or just visiting. If there were any animal babies to be born, Jimmy was able to witness these miracles. Those were happy times. Vergie and Claude never had any children, and Jimmy more than filled that void each summer.

Saturday nights were a big thing in that part of the country, as the families of the farmers, farm hands and ranchers went in to Osceola and mingled around the square visiting, usually ending up at the movie house to see Gene Autry, Tom Mix or Roy Rogers. The stores remained open so the women could shop for dry goods and groceries, while the men got their hardware and other items. Jimmy bought her Levi jeans at the one and only dry goods store for 98 cents a pair. Her friends in Osceola were Betty and Lucille Brown, whose father owned the drugstore with the soda fountain, and Peggy Parker whose family was in the banking business there. Brown's Drugstore was a meeting place for everyone. Roe thoroughly enjoyed going there to play the pinball machines, always trying to beat Fred Brown. Fred made Margaret the best fountain coke, and Jimmy was allowed to go behind the fountain and make her own concoctions, which were quite original. Usually Margaret would let Jimmy invite various friends to spend some part of the summer at the ranch, at which time it never got dull, as

Ozark ranch life was all new to them, and they had a lot to learn, to see and do. Jimmy enjoyed each summer and always felt she had the best of two worlds — country girl in the summer and city gal in the winter.

Boy Scouting Flourished

The first office I remember was a big old rambling house at 3215 Park Avenue. It had a wide winding staircase which was fun to run up and down. The office was moved there in 1930 and in 1933 to 1937 was located at 410 Land Bank Building. Wanting larger quarters, they moved upstairs to 510 Land Bank Building which was located at 10th and Baltimore.

June 23, 1933, the National Council Meeting of the Boy Scouts of America was held in Kansas City. Seven thousand boys reenacted the Council Boy Scout Round-up which had been held earlier. Dr. James E. West, Chief Scout Executive of the U.S.A., was so impressed by the tremendous event that he suggested every council in the U.S.A. should have such an activity. The council also presented 311 young men who received their Eagle award from the hands of Daniel Beard, one of the founders of Scouting in America.

Roe planned many Scouter parties which involved them and their entire families. These were usually costume parties, as Roe never wanted anyone to feel inferior, thereby wearing a costume was fun, and there was no reason for remaining at home because one might feel they had nothing proper or good enough to wear. These parties were always fun, and marvelous fellowship always developed.

Margaret's Life

Margaret felt she had to make a life for herself, as Roe was so involved in Boy Scouting, civic organizations and other youth work that little time was spent on the homefront. She went back to her theatre work. She worked on scenery, as well as being an actress in many, many plays throughout the years. She worked in the Jewish Theatre, Children's Community Theatre, Civic Theatre, actually any and all that had productions in the offing. She would read the script twice and know her part, as well as all the other parts. She made quite a name for herself. Enjoying all this, Margaret enrolled Jimmy to take elocution lessons from Lenore Anthony, whose studio was at 3000 Campbell. Jimmy could ride the streetcar to get there and back. This really was not Jimmy's "cup of tea." Where Margaret could memorize with no problem, Jimmy could never memorize. She would ad lib her way through all readings, parts in plays and whatever else that came about. She could speak from the heart and mind, but not in the words of another individual. That quirk followed her all through life. Making talks and/or speeches was no problem, as she spoke what she knew and what she felt.

The year 1936 was rough for Roe. His mother Ada had been in ill health for some time, and her health worsened as the year progressed. The last month of her life, Margaret and Roe took turns driving to Richmond, Missouri, where Sam was minister of the Presbyterian Church. Margaret usually stayed with Ada during the day while Jimmy was in school, and Roe took over the night shift. Ada had had more influence on Roe than any other individual in his life. No one could compare to her in his eye. She was the one who helped him set his goals in life, and he strived to please her at all times. It was very hard on Roe watching his mother gradually slip away from him, and there was nothing he could do to make her better. He cherished their visits, held her hand, and reassured her of his love and devotion each evening.

The phone rang early one morning, and Margaret had a feeling this was the call to inform her and Jimmy that Ada had passed away during the night and met her Maker. Roe could hardly talk. Margaret left immediately for Richmond to assist him. Jimmy went on to school. Upon their return, Margaret went to the school and got Jimmy out, as she knew the sunshine she gave her dad would be the best medicine for Roe at that time. It was decided that they would just have a snack for dinner that evening, as no one really felt like eating much. Before they could eat, the doorbell rang, and it was Margaret's uncle from Canada, along with his wife and five children. They had not given any previous notice; therefore Margaret had to inform them of the death in the family, and of the people who would be arriving to stay at the house. With that, they took off for Kentucky, and Margaret called the relatives they were heading for to warn them of their arrival in a day or two.

The day of the funeral was a long one, as a service was held in the church in Richmond, followed by the long, slow drive back to Kansas City behind the hearse to Central Presbyterian Church, and later to the Forest Hill Mausoleum for Ada's internment. Jimmy never left Roe's side throughout the day and sat with him in the limousine. Margaret tried to protect Roe from the crowd, as everyone wanted to talk with him, and he preferred not to do so until the following day after a night's rest, as he was completely exhausted.

Ada's funeral was the first for Jimmy. She had gone back to Kentucky with Margaret when James Rains was critically ill and passed away, and not yet being eight years old at the time, she was invited to a friend's house to play for the afternoon. Ada and Sam were very close to Jimmy, and it was hard for her to believe that she and her grandmother could no longer do beadwork and other handwork again. She was the one who taught Jimmy all those beautiful and cherished talents which she kept up all through her life.

Life settled down once again, and everyone got back to the ol' routine. Margaret kept busy in the theatre, at times working with college students. She became president of nearly every organization she joined, which over the years was quite a variety. She was a P.E.O., joined Ladies of Rotary, Woman's City Club, Kansas City Young Matrons, Kansas City Rose Society, Kansas City Museum, Salvation Army and Saddle and Sirloin, which was her favorite. She and Roe belonged to the club, but Margaret was the rider in the family. She enjoyed her horse, horseback riding and being able to participate in the American Royal. She and Roe led very busy, active and worthwhile lives, always working toward the betterment of their city and fellow man.

Jimmy always said she was the original "home alone" kid, as she would come home from school, change clothes, play outside a while, practice the piano, have a bite to eat, do homework, take a bath and go to bed. It was a way of life and never bothered her, as all the neighbors were aware, and if she needed anything they were the first to offer. Even though doors were never locked and often left open, she was never afraid. Margaret usually left notes for her, and Jimmy always knew where and how to get in touch with her mother if necessary.

Time Marches On

It almost seems ordained that Don Baldwin, the first greeter to the Bartle family upon their arrival in St. Joseph, ended up being the first boy called into the Tribe of Mic-O-Say at the St. Joseph camp, became camp director at Osceola in 1935, and in 1939 became the Tribe's first Acting Chieftain. In 1937 Judge E.E. Kirkland joined the staff and worked with Don in the rural district. In 1940 Don left Kansas City and became the Scout Executive of the San Angelo, Texas Council. In years to come he would become the Executive of the Kansas City, Kansas Council. Jimmy has always been very proud of her first baby sitter with all of his accomplishments, and of having him as a treasured friend through the years. Roe had truly influenced this young man's life.

Boy Scouting had grown by leaps and bounds under Roe's direction. In 1937 there were 3,429 boys in the summer camp. Six leaders and 71 boys attended the National Jamboree in Washington, D.C.

Summer of 1937 was a big change for the Bartle clan. Rotary International was held in Nice, France, and Roe was a keynote speaker. Margaret and Roe decided to take Jimmy out of school so she too could make the trip. Jimmy was excited about such a wonderful trip, plus the fact it meant she would not have to take any of her finals at school. She was to graduate from the seventh grade that June. Kansas City did not have an eighth grade in the elementary schools. Pupils went straight from seventh grade to attend four years of high school. Shopping for the trip was fun and furious. All was in readiness on time.

Margaret and Roe would travel together, while Granddad Sam and Jimmy would be travel mates. What a marvelous childhood memory this trip made for Jimmy!

Margaret, Jimmy and Sam drove to New York by way of Kentucky to see all of Margaret's family and to visit other points of interest along the way. Roe had taken the train to New York, where all four met and had a few days visiting the big city. They left for Europe on the Cunard White Star Line ship, S.S. Carinthia, that had been chartered by Rotary International. It was great fun to be able to wander all over the ship and do any and everything one could imagine. Margaret and Roe were on "A" deck, and upon arrival in their room found over a dozen arrangements of flowers sent by friends and well wishers, as well as baskets of fruit, numerous letters and telegrams. Margaret could not remember when she had ever been so excited. Jimmy and Sam were on "C" deck, and to Jimmy's delight, she had a corsage awaiting her, as well as a few telegrams. It was great meeting Rotarians from all over the United States. With many children aboard it was a very active voyage. The two adults who impressed Jimmy the most were Paul Harris, the founder of Rotary, and Bernie Vessey. They were always working up a sing-along, and many new songs were learned and enjoyed. Seeing the two gentlemen together was a sight, as Paul Harris was a tall, distinguished man, and Bernie Vessey was of small stature and very lovable.

It took 10 days to reach Cherbourg, France. From that point, they took a train to Paris where they spent the night. The following day was an eight-hour train ride to Nice. The scenery was beautiful. Margaret and Roe got settled in their room, and Jimmy and Sam in theirs. It was a busy time for all. Margaret and Roe had meetings to attend, receptions and the like. Sam, too, had meetings; therefore, much to Jimmy's delight, she had a lot of free time during those few days and made good time seeing all of Nice and shopping for little items to take home to her friends. The day the President of France was due to arrive at the hotel for lunch, Jimmy had been out shopping and was just returning to the hotel on the run, when all at once she was surrounded by soldiers with bayonets. Scared to death, she did her best to explain she was an American Rotary daughter, and she was due to lunch with her grandpere. Her French came through in fine shape as they seemed to understand, and she was released to go on to the hotel. It seems even in 1937 the European countries felt a war might be imminent; therefore, chances were not taken with their Heads of State. Roe always felt his speech at the Rotary conference was the worst he ever made, the reason being it had to be written out and he was to read it. All talks were translated and printed in French, German, Chinese, English, Italian, etc. Roe had not read a speech since elementary school days, and his thoughts went faster than his eyes. Nonetheless, he made it through in fine shape and was relieved to get that behind him.

At the close of the conference, Margaret and Roe were joined by Elizabeth and Joyce Hall for a limousine side trip to Montreaux, Zurich, Interlaken and Lucerne. They were all very impressed with the beautiful scenery, clean country, healthy people and wonderful vegetable and flower gardens. At the completion of their trip, Roe bid Margaret good-bye and returned to the states, as he had a lot of work and projects he wanted to accomplish. Margaret joined another group of Rotarians and spent many weeks traveling through France, Switzerland, Italy and Germany, before moving on to London.

Jimmy and Sam left Nice for a few days in Paris, then on to the United Kingdom where he had such joy showing Jimmy the land of his childhood and introducing her, as well as showing her off to his relatives all over the island. It was wonderful for Jimmy to see and stay in their homes and learn their way of life. It was hard to sleep, as there was too much to see and sleeping was a waste of time as far as she was concerned. When it came time to return to London, Jimmy had mixed feelings. She felt she could live there and enjoy their way of life also, but it was now time to catch the train to London where Sam would be taking Jimmy to a reception by the Duke of Kent.

After getting settled at the Royal Hotel, Woburn Place, Russell Square in London, Sam was ready for a rest, so once again Jimmy went out and about shopping and seeing the sights. The following evening was the reception. It was the one and only time she wore a fancy dubonnet taffeta ankle-length dress with white anklets and dainty brown suede sandals. The reception was held in Guild Hall and, of course, it was a magnificent evening for Jimmy. Sam had informed her she had better have her very best manners that evening and do as he said, when he said it. After being greeted, they milled around visiting various people in attendance. Jimmy was fascinated with the Duke of Kent. He looked like a "dream prince" to her. She kept an eye on him and, after some time, she noticed he, too, was keeping an eye on her. She was the only child in attendance at this reception. The Duke came over and asked Jimmy if he could show her around Guild Hall. She was almost tongue-tied but accepted graciously. The Duke took her all over, including down to the dungeon, telling her stories all along the way. What an evening for a 12-year-old! Upon return to the hotel, Sam could hardly wait to get to bed, but not Jimmy. Sam told her folks later that he felt she did not sleep a wink that night, remembering the excitement.

Once Margaret arrived in London, Sam took her to Cornwall to meet some of the folks down in the "tin country" and on down to Land's End. Even though it had been months, time passed all too fast, and it was soon time to return home.

The return trip was made on the Anchor Line S.S. Transylvania. Being regular passengers, they had to stay within their appointed assignments. The one thing Jimmy will never forget was all the food served aboard the ships. Breakfast, mid-morning soup, lunch, afternoon tea, dinner and midnight snack. All the food was delicious and served in a very attractive manner. Sam was the one who enjoyed the food the most, and Jimmy could hardly wait until lunch and dinner each day to see what Sam would select. It was noted that he chose several meats, and when it came time for dessert, he chose one of each and loved every bite. It was a joy to see someone receive such pleasure from his meals.

Back to the states, passing the Statue of Liberty and being greeted by friends made for an impressive arrival. After visiting friends in South Orange, New Jersey, they drove back to Kansas City via a northern route to see friends and relatives along the way.

Sam remained in Kansas City a few days before returning to Richmond. Everyone had a hard time settling down after such an interesting, historic, informative and educational trip, filled with memories that would last a lifetime.

New Horizons

Once settled back home, Margaret had to get Jimmy prepared for school. She and Roe had discussed the matter and decided she was too young to go straight on to four years of high school. They enrolled Jimmy in the eighth grade at Sunset Hill School for Girls at 51st and Wornall Road. This was quite a change for Jimmy and rather difficult for her to adjust. Roe had instilled in his daughter her beliefs, way of handling people and her outlook on life. She made up her mind that the other students would have to accept her as she was, as she was just plain Jimmy, down to earth, and would not be changing.

While the rest of his family was seeing all the sights, Roe was back holding the fort, and the Scouting program was making more headlines due to their activities. The 18th annual Round-up was held in the American Royal Building and the first Boy Scout Round-up to be held in the new Municipal Auditorium was on May 8-9, 1936.

A clothing drive was held to help southeast Missouri flood victims in the fall of 1937. The boys collected a total of 492,027 garments.

The Forties Roll In

Jimmy witnessed, even as a small child, the brotherhood of Boy Scouting, plus the quality of life needed to be a healthy, honest, upright citizen, as well as a Christian. Roe was such a fabulous model for the youth of Kansas City, but no finer, more fair, understanding and loving father could be had than Roe Bartle. His hours may have been long and his time short on the homefront, but he was always there when Jimmy really needed him, and he answered every question she ever asked, plus some she did not ask. She was taught to stand up for her own ideas, express her beliefs and follow through, always with a positive outlook. All duties must be fulfilled. The truth might hurt, but you never lied, and if the truth hurt, that was the other person's problem. He set her values for life. Another thing Jimmy learned was the fact that you cannot and should not stop progress or change. That is one of the things our country was built on — constant change. Dreams can come true, and we can be different.

Roe and Jimmy had a very special relationship. Any real problems, whether personal, school or anything else, he would advise her and guide her down the proper path. Many marvelous lessons were learned in the years that followed, troubled years, war years, a whole new and different world to challenge, or be challenged.

Schools in the '40s had problems with smoking, chewing gum, talking and running through the halls. Very different from the problems in the years to come.

The later thirties and early forties were years that Jimmy and Roe became very close. All the times that Jimmy and Roe spent together were deeply cherished by both parties. No daughter spent less time with a father, but felt closer to a father than Jimmy. The time she had with her father was prime time.

Roe's Rotary Club had a family picnic at Unity Farm every year. It was a special fun time for Jimmy and Roe. There was a father-daughter dance contest each year, and Jimmy and Roe won first place four years in a row. Roe was a fantastic dancer, light on his feet, and could guide a partner with ease. He was proud he and his daughter were able to win the main prize.

Another prized time for Jimmy and Roe was during the winter months when Roe would want to go down to the ranch and check things out. Margaret had no interest in going down in the wintertime, but Jimmy was always ready. Roe would come home and ask Jimmy if she was interested in going to the ranch for the weekend, and if she could be ready in five minutes, she could go with him. She was always packed and ready to go. Upon arrival at the ranch they would put out all the vegetables they had brought from the city, and they would make what Roe called Mulligan stew. It was a marvelous meal for such a weekend, as they would eat it for breakfast, lunch and dinner each day until they returned to the city. Jimmy would have an enjoyable weekend riding her horse and visiting with Vergie, while Roe would drive his big Buick across the fields and sit there by the hour studying his white-faced Herefords. My, how he loved his cattle, as well as every other aspect of the ranch. He loved being a gentleman farmer, but Margaret really wanted no part of ranching, other than horseback riding. This was not her way of life. She preferred the big city life and society as a whole. Jimmy could have lived at the ranch and been happy doing so. She loved this way of life and the wholesome people she got involved with each summer.

Roe took Jimmy to Camp White, located at 120th and Blue Ridge Road, with him one winter day while he inspected the camp and checked through on some details. On this visit there was a new horse there, and Jimmy asked permission to ride the horse. Knowing what a good horsewoman she was, Roe gave his permission. Jimmy rode down the hill with Roe following in the Buick. At one point the horse vaulted very unexpectedly, and Jimmy went rolling off down the hill. Roe whizzed down the hill, jumped out of his car, and ran to his daughter lying on the ground. Jimmy had been knocked out but gradually came to, and all was well. No broken bones, just her pride was hurt, but it was two months before they found the horse again on a farm several miles down the road.

Jimmy loved to go with her dad to the father-daughter-son luncheon held with his Rotary Club. That was always a very special time. She had her father all to herself. Another time that was special was the Christmas luncheon Roe had for all his employees. He had a lovely luncheon at the Hotel Muehlebach with all his employees and their spouses in attendance. It was their big happy family. The food was outstanding, entertainment great, and Roe always gave his people a bonus from the money he made in making speeches throughout the year. He felt they all deserved such, as they carried on the business of the day while he was away speaking on Boy Scouting and/or Kansas City.

Christmas Eve was another special time for Roe and Jimmy. Each year Roe wanted everyone to have a memorable Christmas. He always tried to remember everyone. He had great joy in shopping for the great variety of gifts involved. His gals at the office spent evenings wrapping all the presents, and then on Christmas Eve he and Jimmy would drive all over the city delivering them. Usually it was after 2 a.m. before they got back home. As a rule, Jimmy would deliver the gift or gifts, then they would move on to the next place, but some places they would go in and visit a while. The Catholic friends were usually left until last as they were always up having their tree. The Charles Aylward family was usually the last family visited before going home and dropping into bed.

Speaking of Christmas, it might be noted that Roe got up each Christmas morning and left the house, not returning until late afternoon. He would be out checking the Boys' Home, orphanages, the city jail, and other places he felt no one would remember but he and God. He always wanted to make sure everyone had something to be thankful for on Christmas Day.

Back home on Christmas, there were all the widows, widowers, old maids and bachelors sitting around the dinner table. Jimmy always felt this was her holiday family, because all the relatives were too far away to be there with them. Not having relatives close, she called each of these individuals either Aunt or Uncle "So and So." They were her family, and she loved them all.

"The Last Days of Pompeii" playing at the Mainstreet Theater was the last movie to which Roe took Jimmy. He was so busy telling her about how the crumbling walls were made of cardboard boxes and the horses thrown over the wall by the blasts were stuffed animals, etc., to the extent she told him to please be quiet, as she was crying and enjoying herself. She loved to live every movie she saw, but Roe was disturbed because his daughter was getting emotional over a movie.

Roe was a public person; therefore, time spent with his family was always very precious and prized. He and Jimmy had a very special relationship, a mutual admiration society. She often would stay up until 2 a.m. to have a chat with him, even though he would arrive home dead tired. They would sit on her bed and talk things out. No task was ever too small nor a challenge too great. Roe's constant mission in life was to give himself away with a prayer always for others, and no matter the time, he always made time for his Jimmy.

An Addition to the Family

September 1939, the United Kingdom entered the second World War. Roe had two precious little cousins living 20 miles south of London. He could not help but think of them and wonder what might happen to them during the bombings by the Germans. Margaret and Roe wrote to the cousins' parents, Gwyn and Gordon Brown, asking permission to bring the children to the states for the duration of the war, where they could grow up safely. It took many months, much paper work, and investigation on both sides of the Atlantic before they could really get the ball rolling. Finally, an English lady was secured who wanted to get to the states and was willing to bring the children over if Roe would pay her way. Roe paid her way, plus a month in Lisbon for all three, before they took another ship and made their way on to New York. The children arrived in Kansas City by air on a very hot Missouri day in June. They were wearing several sets of wool shorts and shirts and had very little luggage. Not being used to the heat, they were soon ushered to the car and off for our house. Jennifer was 12 that April before her arrival, and Denis celebrated his eighth birthday on that July 8th. What fun Margaret had with them! The following day they went downtown to John Taylor Dry Goods Store, where Mrs. James took care of the challenge of outfitting these children for the summer. Jen and Den were excited over all their new wardrobe and felt indeed very fortunate to be in the states with Uncle Roe, Aunt Margaret and Jimmy.

During the first meal, with the whole new family together around the dining table, sirens could be heard going down Main Street. Much to the surprise of Margaret, Jimmy and Roe, there were two small children ejecting from their chairs to the floor. They thought we were going to have an air raid and dropped to the floor under the table for protection.

It was a blessing that everyone went to Osceola for the summer. Being in the Ozarks gave the children time to relax, get accustomed to American ways and customs, put their fears behind them and live as children should be able to live.

For the first time in her life Jimmy had to share a room, her free time, share ration coupons, and she also became the main sitter for the cousins. She could not accept all invitations that came to her, as she had to stay home and take care of the children or take them some place they had been invited. She had been used to sharing but not quite so much!

The second summer Jen and Den were in the states, Margaret left them completely in Jimmy's charge, while she took off for Arizona and California for the summer. Jimmy was a disciplinarian. She wanted to be firm and teach these children right from wrong. Jennifer and Jimmy had a rough time at it, as Jennifer had a problem that Jimmy was determined to whip (being personal we will not mention what the problem was). It took perseverance and the whole summer for Jimmy to accomplish her mission — one that Margaret could not correct during the previous year. Jennifer was not too happy with this older cousin who deprived her of much throughout those summer months as her punishment.

The children were enrolled in J.C. Nichols Elementary School, and Roe soon realized they needed a little special education, and therefore sent Jennifer to Sunset Hill and Denis to Pembroke Country Day, as he felt they needed particular help in math, changing pounds and pence to dollars and cents, plus a broader view on history. Jennifer, as her choice, attended Southwest High School a couple of years before returning home, but Denis remained at Country Day. Jennifer took piano lessons and did well. She joined the Girl Scouts, while Denis joined Cub Scouts and later Boy Scouts. Memories from their four-plus years are very interesting and rewarding.

Roe had been given a St. Bernard when attending a conference at the University of Indiana. His name was Indiana Thibodeau VI. When the dog first entered the house, Margaret thought Roe had brought home a calf from the ranch. Thibby was a loving, playful dog, and Margaret felt him entirely too big to keep in the house. When she had him chained in the backyard and he heard the school children out at recess, he invariably broke loose and ended up on the playground. Many times Jimmy and a fellow student named Arthur would have to take him home and rush back to school. When the British children arrived, Margaret insisted that Thibby be sent to the ranch where he would have more room to roam and more to eat since he was supposed to have 10 pounds of dog food a day. Meat being rationed made his former diet impossible, and the ranch soon became his new home.

Doing Their Share

Due to the fact Jennifer and Denis were not American citizens, they were not issued ration books of any kind. This made it rough, especially on the shoe ration books. Their feet were still growing, and a need for larger sizes became apparent. In addition, Roe had to special order his high top shoes, and that took twice the coupons required for a regular pair. Margaret used all of Jimmy's shoe coupons for the children to the point where Jimmy thought she might go barefooted before the war was over!

Margaret used a lot of sugar as she did a lot of canning during the war years, so everyone learned to drink their tea and coffee without sugar. Actually she was allowed extra sugar for canning; it was not enough. Most of the canning was done during the summer months at the ranch. Having the ranch, we were allowed to have "C" gasoline ration coupons in order to run the tractors and other implements. Margaret had her regular "A" gas coupon book, and Roe had extra for his various responsibilities. Seldom were they found short on gasoline, but they were very careful how they used their supply. Margaret and the children rode the streetcar or bus whenever possible. Those were rough times, and yet some of the best of times, as everybody always pulled together, most made their own fun, and all were working for the cause.

Margaret became a nurse's aide at Trinity Hospital, and at one time during the war when there was a shortage of doctors, she helped deliver a couple of babies. She worked with the Red Cross, taught first aid classes and helped on other related projects when called upon.

John Thornberry was in charge of the Kansas City Canteen where Jimmy and her best friend, Bette Ruth Rice, worked during their free hours. They met many young service men there. Their dancing improved a lot due to the fact they danced several times a week with soldiers and sailors from all over the country. They found out dancing styles were definitely different and soon could recognize what part of the country the men were from by the way they danced.

Royal Air Force men came in from Miami and Ponca City, Oklahoma, when they had a weekend leave. Because of Jennifer and Denis being with her, Jimmy met many of these men and invited several of them home. The children loved seeing people from their homeland. Another country represented was France. The French Air Force brought men over from Algiers, where they had come together after their escape from the Germans. The Kansas City Canteen was their first introduction to Americans, and American women. They, too, were most interesting, and Jimmy got to practice her French a lot in speaking, as well as writing letters. Margaret and Roe enjoyed having all these young men in their home. They found them most interesting, hearing the various tales the men had to spin for them, and offered them whatever courtesies possible. It was very educational for one and all, plus making some life-long friends for Jimmy.

Regarding the war effort, Roe was the executive director of American War Dads and expanded it from an area organization to a national one, but he always refused to accept a salary.

With so many of his young Boy Scouts and Mic-O-Say tribesmen in the service, he had his Girl Friday, Margaret Halstead, keep a round robin letter going out each month to those for whom they had addresses. In turn, the fellows would write back, and she was able to pass on messages to others. Through her letters, many found hometown buddies in the next village, in a hospital they could visit, or enabled them to write their own letters to friends. Margaret's letters were extremely popular during the war and became very famous before the war was over. They were like a visit from home.

The Boy Scouts were doing their share for the war

effort by volunteering to help on first aid, fire prevention, growing "victory gardens," helping farmers bring crops in at harvest time, and volunteering to staff plane-spotter posts. They gathered hundreds of thousands of pounds of scrap iron, aluminum, rubber and waste paper. Paper drives were a weekly occurrence. They sold War Bonds, helped the Blood Bank and gathered books to be sent overseas to servicemen. Many who had been Sea Scouts were great candidates for the Navy. The Kansas City Area Boy Scouts made very impressive records throughout the various branches of the service. Roe was more than proud of all "his boys." When one was lost, his heart was heavy laden, and he would be one of the first to contact the parents, offering his assistance as needed.

All down through the years, there was never a need for an ambulance at Scout camp, as Roe took that upon himself. No one ever made better time down the highway between Osceola and Kansas City than Roe. The closest run he ever made was taking a young Scout from camp to St. Luke's Hospital with a hot appendix. They arrived barely in time, and all went well. There was never a boy in jeopardy, and as long as the Chief was in charge, the boys relaxed and knew all would be okay.

Jimmy graduated from high school June 6, 1942. She always knew her father would not be able to attend her graduation ceremony, as his speaking engagements were booked a good three years in advance. Therefore, he was addressing another graduating class at the time she received her diploma. She had grown up sharing her dad with "the world" and fully understood. She was grateful her mother could be in attendance, but mainly she was just thankful to get out of high school and have one more wonderful summer at the ranch before having to enter college in the fall.

That summer was the last time Jimmy had a chance to see and visit with a lot of the fellows she had grown up with and who had been on staff at Boy Scout camp for several years. She would be going to college while they would be going off to war.

Before Joe Hunt left for the service, Roe had purchased his Chevy coupe so Jimmy would have transportation and could care for the British children during the summer months. Margaret had planned to be elsewhere.

It was a great summer, enjoyed by all, and memories prized. Jimmy had a dear friend, Harriett Smith, who lived behind her on 69th Street. Harriett had gone to the ranch several summers but did not have the best of luck. The first summer she went home with pneumonia due to hay seed in her lungs from pitching hay in the loft. The following summer she went out in the back pasture to tell all the colts and horses good-bye, only to have the Shetland pony come up to her while she was in the saddle of a larger horse and bite her on the leg. Harriett ended up in the hospital in Kansas City upon her return home, and carried those scars to the end of her life. While visiting Jimmy and making trips over to Scout camp, Jimmy introduced Harriett to Joe Hunt. You might say that Jimmy became a match maker, as Harriett and Joe went together the years left in high school and during their college years. It was decided they would be married on a weekend leave before Joe reported for active duty. That they did, and George Charno gave them their honeymoon at the Hotel Muehlebach. When Joe returned home from the European theater after the war, Harriett introduced him to their daughter Cathey.

There were many, many other fellows who went off

to war after that summer. Jimmy tried to keep in contact with a lot of them and passed the news on to Margaret Halstead so she could add information to her "round robin" letters. When Jimmy came home on the bus, the Bartle postman was usually on that bus and would fill her in on who all she had heard from that particular day.

Also, that last summer Eldon Newcomb called over to the ranch to see if Jimmy might assist him in catching some insects down in the valley at Boy Scout camp and later mount them for display. She was delighted that he called her and drove over from the ranch to help him. She parked and dashed on down in the valley, only to find when she arrived there, Professor Newcomb told her to dash back up to the swimming pool and jump in. At first she wondered what on earth was going on, but with a glance she saw that she was covered from head to toe with newly hatched ticks. Minus her shoes, she jumped in the pool, then dashed to her car and returned to the ranch where Myrtle, the cook-maid, checked her over to make sure she was free of the pests.

Roe permitted Jimmy to go to the Nature Lodge and assist in making displays for teaching and viewing by the visitors and guests. She loved this. It was something she really enjoyed doing and was afraid of little or nothing. On a Sunday visiting day she was working in the Nature Lodge and had taken a bull snake out of the cage. She heard a hissing sound and thought it was a rattler loose, so dropped the six-foot-long bull snake, only to see all the visitors evacuate with speed. She truly felt badly about this, especially when she realized that the sound had come from the bull snake and all the other reptiles were secured in fine shape.

Come fall, Margaret was busy trying to get her

daughter ready for college. Jimmy had received a scholarship to Lindenwood College, a Presbyterian woman's college located in St. Charles, Missouri. Roe had very mixed feelings about Jimmy leaving for college. She had wanted to go to the University of Texas or the University of Arizona, but Roe felt those educational institutions were too far away from home. It was left up to Margaret to drive Jimmy to St. Charles and get her daughter settled at Lindenwood. The car was as fully loaded as possible, and Jimmy swore she needed each and every item contained therein. The drive back to Kansas City seemed extra long to Margaret, and once home she felt an empty feeling. She was grateful Jen and Den were there, as they kept her very busy, leaving her little time to sit around and miss her Jimmy.

During the school year, Roe stopped by the campus several times on his return trips to Kansas City from various speaking engagements. One of these times, Jimmy and five of her fellow students had signed out to go in to St. Louis to a circus. Roe visited with all of them much longer than any of them planned, and Jimmy asked him to take them to the bus station. Upon arrival, they learned the bus had already left, so she asked her dad to try to catch the bus down the highway, which he did. They arrived in St. Louis after dark, and being much later than they had planned, they decided to go to the Mayfair Hotel and have dinner, go to a movie, and then back to the campus. While eating their dinner, the house mother walked in with her date and spied them immediately. They were informed to return to the campus immediately and to check in with her first thing the following morning. All were very disappointed but did as instructed. The following morning they reported to the house mother who promptly sent them to the dean. Jimmy was the last to be interviewed about the previous evening and was informed they must have memorized their speeches, as they all said the same thing. A decision was made — all six girls were to be campused for six weeks since they did not go where they had signed out to be.

Some two months later, Roe returned to the campus for another visit with Jimmy. On this visit, Jimmy asked Roe to please come with her as she wanted to introduce him to the dean, and he came along. When they entered the dean's office, Jimmy introduced her father as the man who got her and her friends campused for six weeks after his visit, making it too late for them to attend the circus, and no one had believed their story. The dean was really embarrassed and could not apologize enough. Jimmy got a big kick out of this, as did Roe. He felt badly that the girls had been campused, but it did not really bother any of them, as they left the campus after dark if they really needed something.

Jimmy made many wonderful friends at college, but did not wish to return. She wanted to become a doctor and felt that this was not a satisfactory place to get her education. Having decided not to return in the fall, Jimmy enrolled in Huff Business College, thinking she would remain just long enough so she would not have to attend a regular college. Much to her surprise, she thoroughly enjoyed the full business course. She became a stenographist, graduating with honors. She was president of Alpha Iota, the business sorority, and was pleased and proud of her record.

She wanted to secure a job on her own, but Roe insisted she work for him first. Jimmy informed him she would work at the office, but she would not take his dictation, as he dictated 350 words a minute, that being faster than she desired.

Jimmy enjoyed working at the Boy Scout office, but wanted to get out on her own. Roe was out of the office one day when Jimmy received a phone call from a friend asking if she could leave for an interview with a gentleman with T.W.A. who needed a secretary pronto. She jumped at the chance, leaving the office immediately. Upon completion of the interview, Don Heter asked Jimmy if she could start work the following morning. She informed him that her father was on a speaking tour for Rotary, and her parents had planned on traveling the state the following week. Since she was working for her father, it had been agreed upon that she would remain at home all week taking care of her English cousins for them. She felt due to her situation she would never be hired, but Mr. Heter told her he would look forward to her arriving at the office at 8 a.m. a week from Monday. Jimmy could not believe she had been hired, as she had never applied for a position.

When Margaret and Roe returned from their Rotary trip, Jimmy informed them of her new position. Roe could hardly believe his ears. He had Margaret set the alarm so he could take her to work each morning, making sure she would be on time. After the first week, Jimmy informed her dad she could make it on her own, and thanked him for his concern. It was hard for Roe to accept, but he complied.

The Mighty Staff

Roe had the greatest staff of any Boy Scout Council in the United States. If he had not had such an excellent staff, he would never have been able to leave town so much to make speeches, attend meetings, conferences, training sessions and other types of business. He always knew when he left, things would go on as usual, as all his employees were responsible and efficient in every way.

Ernie Modlin and "Doc" Soule were aboard before Roe came to Kansas City, and he was proud to keep them on his staff. From St. Joseph, as time progressed, he added Joseph Scanlon and Byron Hunt.

After Don Baldwin, the new camp director was Joe Macy. Chuck Henion was number one in teaching Indian lore and all the authentic Indian dances, plus the making of the headdresses and costumes.

Jimmy felt the most spectacular Boy Scout Round-up was the year John Modlin, son of Ernie, performed the Indian dance, and started by coming down from the ceiling of the Municipal Auditorium. It was awesome and a spectacular performance to be remembered a lifetime. Chuck Henion taught him well. Kansas City had the most outstanding Round-up of all the councils in the country. The men from the national office tried to work their schedule to be in Kansas City at the time of one or both evenings. It was definitely the best show in town.

Jack Armstrong was added to the staff around 1940. He and his bride, Libby, came to Kansas City following their honeymoon in order for Jack to begin his career as a professional Scouter. Roe was a great influence on this young man, guiding his professional career throughout his life.

All of Roe's office employees were loyal and worked long, hard hours to make sure all projects were completed. Laura Mehrbacher was his first secretary. When she had to move on, Roe hired a brilliant young and talented college graduate by the name of Margaret Halstead. She became his main "Girl Friday." She knew Roe's business and saw that all ran smoothly for the Chief. Just keeping his calendar, making his train, plane and hotel reservations down through the years would have been enough of a task in itself, as Roe traveled over a million miles a year for over 40 years. After WW II, she was affectionately known as "Mother Superior."

There was a period when Roe had two male stenos, making it convenient to have them travel with him when he drove around the state making speeches. He could dictate going down the road, meaning his desk would not pile extra high with correspondence needing answers when he returned to the city. The two young men were cousins named Harold Petel and Sam Klein. Later they both became court reporters.

To lighten Margaret Halstead's dictation load, Roe hired a young lady right out of high school named Wilma Olson. Wilma was a whizz on the stenograph machine. No matter how fast Roe spoke, she was able to get it all down accurately. She soon became known as "Swede." Both she and Margaret Halstead became well known around the United States, as Roe would refer to them in speeches, and anyone wanting to see, talk or inquire about a speaking engagement would have to go through one or the other.

One day Roe told Margaret and Swede he did not want to see anyone or take any phone calls for a while, as he was trying to make a number of long distance calls involving a project he was working on. A man came in the office and insisted on seeing Roe. They informed the man, "Mr. Bartle is not in. Would you like to make an appointment?" at which point Roe was talking on the phone and raised his voice. The man challenged the girls and informed them they were liars. Roe heard this and came bounding out of his office, grabbed the man by the back of his collar and ushered him to the elevator. His booming voice could be heard on all floors of the Land Bank Building, as he informed the man no one called his employees liars. They were doing as he instructed, and would he kindly never come to his office again. The elevator opened, the man entered, the door closed, and Roe returned to his office to see half the workers in the building had come to that floor to see what was going on. The only other time Roe could remember seeing that man again was when he was in the front row of a conference where Roe was the main speaker, but no reference was ever made to the incident again.

The name Margaret seemed to be a charm for Roe. He was seriously ill one year, having to have a nurse around the clock. No matter where Roe would be, his work went on. Therefore Margaret Halstead came to the house each day to take care of business. Of course, wife Margaret and daughter Margaret (Jimmy) were with him, and then there was a nurse sent to the house to look after him until he could return to the office, whose name was Margaret O'Shannesey. When Roe called out, "Margaret," he had a full force in front of him until we all had to laugh. Nicknames were adopted immediately to solve the situation.

Joe and Jeanne Macy were very close to the Bartle family. Arrival of their twin daughters was exciting for all. Jimmy "baby sat" them from the time of birth until she went off to college. They were precious. When one would cry, the other would sleep. The twins seemed to understand when their time to eat, change of diaper, or time to play would be. It was a joy to take care of them.

Jeanne developed a goiter and would not have an operation due to religious beliefs. Her eyes were about to bulge out of their sockets. Roe was very disturbed. He called Joe into his office and informed him if Jeanne did not enter the hospital over the weekend and have an operation the first of the week, he would be fired. Having the operation saved Jeanne's sight, and in a few weeks all was well.

Roe felt his staff was his family. He worried about each and every one of them and wanted what was best for all concerned.

Back on the Camp Scene

By the end of 1945, the number of Scouts served by the Council had more than doubled — nearly 15,000.

A second Lone Bear Council Ring was badly needed … construction was started, but was first used in 1949. The forties saw over a thousand wearers of Mic-O-Say eagle claws gather each year at the annual tribal feast to greet old friends, pay tribute to those called by the Great Spirit since the last feast, and to honor a new Chieftain selected by the Council of Chieftains.

A badly needed dining hall had been built. Mrs. Annie Lee Parry donated funds for a handicraft lodge. This lodge was constructed during the fall and winter of 1941 and dedicated during the summer of '42. After camp had closed for the summer, Jimmy was still at the ranch. She, along with Vergie and Claude, had gone in to Osceola for a fun evening. They were on their return trip to the ranch when Jimmy told Claude she thought she saw a fire, and it looked as if it were at the camp. Claude drove swiftly to the camp, where they found Parry Lodge in a blazing fire. Jimmy called the Osceola Fire Department, but by the time they arrived it was too far gone. Jimmy stood crying, as it was such a beautiful building and one that was badly needed. The lodge, however, was rebuilt in time for the 1943 summer session.

There were several mainstays at Scout camp. One of those individuals was W.M. "Pappy" Grube ... a grand and wonderful individual. He was handicraft director ... serious and thorough about all he did and taught.

Eb Thresher was the waterfront director and would have no nonsense around the pool. He was delighted to have the pool, as for several years the Scouts and staff swam in the Osage River. (Vergil Owens caught an alligator in the river one year — a story that has never been forgotten.)

In 1948, a new section of the camp was opened called "Sawmill." Scouting was growing and so were the camping facilities.

There were other related camps and camp activities. The Boy Scout staff provided manpower for the Rotary Club camp located near Unity Village where a modified Scouting program was used.

A second Council camp was purchased in 1949. This camp was known as Camp Ernst, and was located about five miles west of Belton, Missouri.

By the end of the forties, there were over 20,000 boys registered. There were 4,239 Scouts who had become Eagles. Kansas City was unmatched with this kind of excellence anywhere in the country. All councils had a challenge, as Kansas City so excelled in all three key areas of leadership, program and membership.

Margaret Roe "Jimmy" Bartle — 1940's

John James Taylor became the beloved son Roe never had.

Excitement on the Home Front

Jimmy had dated numerous young men over a period of years. However, on August 30, 1946 (unforgettable day), she had her first date with a tall, auburn-haired young first generation Scot just discharged from the Air Corps. He had been chased by women during the war and had made up his mind he would not date again — but upon seeing Jimmy at her company picnic, he asked his friends who had accompanied him to the picnic to inquire if Jimmy would accept a date with him. She had been busy trying to break off from another young man, so was very agreeable about accepting a date with him. His name was John James Taylor, a real dream-boat as far as Jimmy was concerned. They dated every night, with Jim picking her up from work and taking her home to change, and returning after he had bathed and changed, to take her to Winstead's for a double cheeseburger, cherry coke and a frosty. They enjoyed each other's company very much and could sit and talk for hours. Jim proposed to Jimmy on September 13, and she accepted. They told no one for a while. They picked out their rings, and during the Cub Show in December they drove down to the auditorium to tell Roe and show her ring to him. He was most pleased, as he too liked this young man. At the same time, he could hardly believe his baby was old enough to get married — the years had flown by.

Margaret had mixed emotions over the news, but it was not long before she got in gear and started planning and giving Jimmy suggestions and ideas for her wedding.

Jimmy turned in her resignation to become effective on January 1, 1947, but T.W.A. would not accept it. The division in which she was employed was in the midst of dissolution. She ended up being everyone's secretary and was relief girl on the big switchboard. She made photostats, did mimeographing and any other chore requested. She tried, however, to inform all that she was leaving April 1 no matter what. The big bosses asked if she would not transfer to another section where she was badly needed and would receive a sizable raise, but she refused all offers.

Roe walked Jimmy down the aisle of Central Presbyterian Church at 8 p.m., April 18, 1947. It was a gorgeous wedding. Hundreds of flowers were all over the packed church and reception hall. It was an exciting evening for everyone. Margaret Halstead sang "Ave Marie," and Joe Macy sang "The Lord's Prayer." The service was recorded, and color movies were made during the reception. Jimmy and Jim took off for the Northwest, and the following morning Margaret and Roe departed for Springfield, Missouri, for a Rotary conference.

The year 1948 was a big year for Roe. He launched the American Humanics Foundation. For over 10 years he had been formulating ideas for the foundation. Having had to hire men for various jobs and not being able to find them, it was his idea to put a course in the colleges to educate students who, upon graduation, would be qualified to cover all phases of youth work. This included raising money, accounting, securing volunteers capable of training young people as well as adults, planning programs, setting up schedules and preparing for all other projects of such a career. The first college to accept the program and add it to their curriculum was Missouri Valley College, located in Marshall, Missouri. It became such a success that the course was expanded to numerous colleges throughout the United States. Graduates from this Humanics major provided prospects for the Boy Scouts, Girl Scouts, Camp Fire Girls, Big Brothers, Big Sisters, boys' clubs, girls' clubs, YMCA, YWCA and other youth-oriented organizations.

A new type of excitement was added to Margaret and Roe's life. Jimmy and Jim were expecting their first child. Roe needed to have teeth extracted and wanted to wait until after the baby arrived. He would call Jimmy every few days to see, "Is today the day?" She finally told her dad to go ahead and take care of his dental work, as she felt he should get that behind him before she gave birth. The baby was due July 4, and July came and went, and still no baby. Roe was thankful he had gotten his dental work done, and he was anxiously awaiting his first grandchild. He called to check each day, as did Margaret. Margaret would give her schedule to Jimmy, so if she was needed she could be contacted. The doctors finally informed Jimmy if the baby did not come by September 1, they would induce labor.

On August 31, 1948 Jim bought a Model A Ford and drove it home to show Jimmy. Upon his arrival, he found her in five-minute labor pains. Jim called Margaret immediately to see if she could take them to the hospital, as he had not had time to check the Model A out and certainly did not want car trouble. Margaret dashed out to 10101 Nall Boulevard and took Jimmy and Jim to St. Luke's Hospital. Roe had arrived, too, and he and Margaret kept Jim company until Pamela Taylor made her appearance at 9:17 p.m. Jim called his folks and told them the news. This being their first granddaughter, they too were excited. Roe wasted no time getting the word out, as it was announced on the front page of the *Kansas City Star* the following morning.

The Fifties

Roe was chairman of the Board when Missouri Valley College needed an interim president. He filled that position from 1948 to 1951. The road was kept hot between Kansas City to Marshall, Missouri, as Roe still fulfilled all his duties and responsibilities as Scout Executive and other obligations in Kansas City.

By the fifties, the Kansas City Area Boy Scout Council had perhaps the strongest council in the country and was admired nationally. A great camping program was provided, and now Camp Osceola was the finest and largest Boy Scout camp in the U.S. Roe always gave credit for the great strides the Council had made during the past 25 years to his outstanding staff and the planning committees.

A reception was held at William Rockhill Nelson Gallery of Art honoring Margaret and Roe on the 25 years. For hours, it was their pleasure to be greeted by Scouts, Scouters, friends, neighbors, the citizens of Kansas City and surrounding towns. It was inspiring to see their eyes sparkle and feel the warmth and abiding friendship everyone held for them.

In commemoration of his many years devoted to his life's dream of building leaders for tomorrow through Boy Scouting, George Charno designed a ring to be presented to Roe. This ring was quite fitting for the large hand that would wear it. An antique European 3-plus carat diamond was placed in the center of a Fleur de Lis design set in platinum. A very outstanding ring which Roe accepted with humility from his board and wore the rest of his life. That ring became a very special heirloom after his death.

The fifties brought forth another granddaughter for the Chief. Sandra Taylor arrived on June 12, 1951. Kansas City had a devastating flood at that time, and not knowing if the water was safe at the Taylor household, Roe sent a truck to the ranch and had many five-gallon milk cans filled with well water and brought back to the city for distribution. He relaxed on that subject once he knew Jimmy could make the baby her formula and the rest of the family could have plenty of fresh water for their consumption.

April 24, 1954, Margaret and Roe became grandparents again to another granddaughter, Dianne Taylor. Margaret and Roe took care of Pam and Sandy while Jimmy was in the hospital and for the first few days at home. They were to bring the girls home to meet their new sister on Friday, May 7, but this was not to be. Very early that morning, Jim called to talk to Roe. Margaret felt something was wrong and dashed to catch Roe before he got out of the driveway. He had planned to go to the office and get several hours of work done before the office opened. He rushed to the phone, only to find Jim just could not talk. Roe said, "Son, if you need me, hang up — if not, speak up." Jim hung the phone up, and Roe left immediately for Johnson County. Neighbors heard him screeching to a halt at Taylor's and felt something was wrong. When Roe walked in, Jim greeted him with the still body of Dianne. Jim was finally able to talk, but Jimmy was in complete shock. Roe got on the phone immediately after he had heard Jim's story. Jim had gone into the nursery to change a diaper and give a bottle to Dianne, letting Jimmy sleep. Then he was going on to his office. Jim had called the doctor the minute he saw Dianne, hoping something could be done. The doctor came, tried everything, and nothing worked, so he left without making any phone calls for them. Roe got on the phone after his arrival, and before long the minister arrived, closest of friends and Ben Roe, Roe's cousin, who took Dianne to the University of Kansas Hospital for an autopsy, before going to the funeral home.

Roe devoted the whole day to Jimmy and Jim. Once he knew Jimmy was under control and surrounded by love, he and Jim took off to all the cemeteries in Kansas City so Jim could purchase the necessary plot. He was very patient, did not rush Jim, and they cried together. Roe told Jim it was hard to understand why the good Lord would take his wee daughter when he wanted and loved his children so dearly. After bringing Jim home, arrangements were discussed and completed. The burial would be the following day at the graveside at Forest Hill Cemetery.

The time that Roe spent with Jimmy and Jim occupied the greater part of the day, but he was where he wanted to be. Once he left the house on Nall, he made double time. Before going downtown, he stopped by his house to check on Margaret and the girls. Margaret was the one who had to break the news to Pam and Sandy and to help them understand the situation at their home. Roe spent time with Margaret and the girls, then grabbed his clothes and dashed to the office. In a few hours he was due at the Municipal Auditorium, where another great performance of the Boy Scout Round-up would commence. Despite the "gray cloud" overhead, the show went on, was fantastic as usual, and everyone tried twice as hard that year to do a top notch job. Friday and Saturday night performances were outstanding. The public extended their hearts, love and sympathy to the Chief and his family. Pam and Sandy did their job of keeping Jimmy so busy she had little time to think of anything but the future.

Down through the years, Roe had instilled in the minds of his Scouts and Scouters that when your family, church, city, county, state or country called upon you, it was your obligation to answer and fulfill that call. While sitting in his office one day, Margaret Halstead entered, informing him several of "his boys" would like to have a conference with him. Roe was delighted to see all of them, and as they were seated around his desk, he began to wonder what was on their minds.

"For a change, Chief, we are here to give you a call. You always told us if an individual was approached to fulfill a duty, it was up to that individual to comply. Kansas City needs honest leadership, by someone who loves their city and desires to see it move forward. We feel and know you are that person. Therefore, we are asking you to please be a candidate for Mayor in the next city election — how about it?" Roe was floored. He had never thought of entering the political world, but there was only one possible answer, and that was Yes. He knew that Scouting and politics did not mix so, of course, he had to resign as the Boy Scout Executive of the Kansas City, Missouri Area Council. Scouting being his first love, this was really a sacrifice on his part.

As was his custom all through life, Roe poured himself into the election, campaigning, leaving "no stone" unturned. With less sleep than usual, he forged ahead, having the time of his life fulfilling his latest challenge.

Margaret had a hard time keeping up with Roe's schedule, having whatever he needed in readiness, and still keeping up with her own schedule. It was indeed a busy household. Margaret made herself available when Roe needed her at his side, or to make a talk or just to drive him somewhere, so he could relax and get his thoughts together along the way.

Jimmy felt rather helpless living out in Johnson County and not really being able to campaign for Roe. The worst was the fact she and Jim would not even be able to vote for him. Her hands were full taking care of her two small daughters, having put the sadness of the past behind her. She was not feeling up to par, but helped Roe in any manner possible when requested.

Election night was more than memorable. It was an evening of excitement like the household had never had before. With such an overpowering victory, telegrams, phone calls, flowers and friends filled their residence.

It was a thrilling day for the family when Roe was sworn in as Mayor of his favorite city in the whole world. Many times down through the years, Roe had been asked to move elsewhere, even to be Chief Scout Executive of the United States, and he turned down all offers, saying, "Kansas City is my city, and here I shall remain."

Roe had been a builder of men through Boy Scouting and American Humanics. He now wanted to build an even better city of Kansas City. He realized he had quite a challenge in front of him, but he was a firm believer in the adage that "hard work never hurt anyone," and he was ready to begin.

Jimmy took the girls down to the City Hall for the swearing in. They were excited and felt so grown up to be in attendance. Their Gran Gran was now Mr. Mayor and they looked forward to returning at a later date to his office on the 29th floor, where he would show them the view of the whole city.

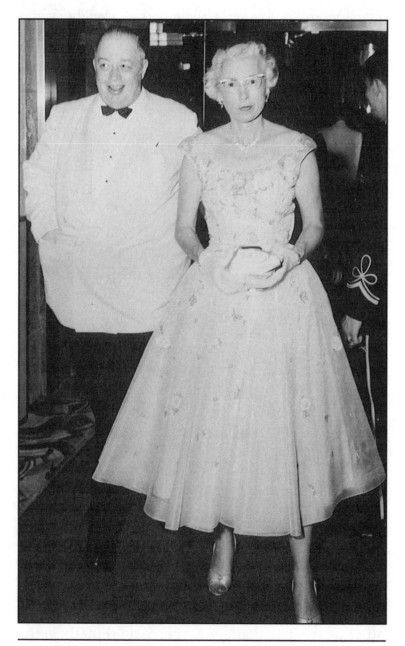

Mr. Mayor and his first lady — Miss Maggie

Mr. Mayor and First Lady

Margaret thought she and Roe had been busy in the past, but now every organization, it seemed, wanted them as guests, to speak, or to present a key to the city. Roe wanted people to be proud of the key to Kansas City; therefore he had special ones made, triple dipped, which were hung on a red, white and blue ribbon. Later he had some made into tie tacs. Because there were many women to be presented with mementos, he had earrings which were very attractive and, of course, delighted the recipients. He also had cuff links made which most men preferred. All had the original "Incorporated 1850" Kansas City seal. He presented a set to Jimmy and Jim, which have also become heirlooms, as Jimmy felt in time they would be collector items and her children would prize them.

Margaret thought Roe worked long hours in the past, but now once again he was working 18 to 20-hour days. He usually went to the office on Saturday and many Sundays after church. She told Roe she never heard of another mayor who worked that kind of hours, but she knew how much he wished to accomplish and indeed did. He was in demand as a speaker more than ever now and was out of town, informing the rest of the nation about his great city. Nothing pleased him more.

Every day brought something different and exciting to Margaret. She usually enjoyed everything she did and was grateful she was still in her prime and full of energy, as she had to change clothes at least three times a day, going from tailored clothes in the morning to formal attire in the evening.

Roe and Margaret often had to divide their time going in separate ways during the evening hours. One evening he gave Margaret five places to go. She informed him, "Never again." She would do two or three stops for him, but that was her limit. At the same time, she reminded him he had a chauffeur, and she had to drive herself, park and walk, while all he had to do was dash in and welcome people, or present a key and leave, but she liked to remain a bit to visit and mingle among the people.

There was so much Roe wanted to do for his city to make it grow and prosper. It was a rough road all the way, as the old political faction had more members on the Council than those presenting the Citizens' ticket. Having only one vote himself, if he could not "brain-wash" a few, it would be a losing vote, the city would suffer, and there was nothing he could do. This was extremely exasperating for Roe. He had always been his own boss,

Swearing in ceremony for Roe's second term as Mayor of Kansas City, Missouri

ran affairs in a positive manner, and this was definitely a whole new experience — a challenge he was hoping to conquer.

Whenever someone is in the spotlight, there always seem to be those who take it upon themselves to heckle, make crazy phone calls and send threatening letters. Roe Bartle was no exception. He received letters even threatening to kill his wife or his daughter, or do away with his grandchildren. Many of these letters were thrown away, but others were directed to the police for follow-up. The police insisted that Roe carry a pistol. When calls came in late at night or the wee hours of the morning, Margaret would usually run downstairs to answer the phone, saying, "Kansas City Police Department," and if it was a crank call, the party would hang up. Margaret always hoped these calls would not wake Roe, as she felt he had enough to worry about without adding this burden. Much of the time, the police followed Margaret home, without her knowledge, and they even patrolled Jimmy's house without her knowing it. It was during this time that Roe insisted they sell their house and move into an apartment.

The house at 25 East 70th was put up for sale, and Margaret was searching a lot of possibilities for an apartment with at least three bedrooms. Finally, they agreed upon the Plaza House at 4712 Roanoke Parkway. The new freeway to downtown was right in front of the building, giving Roe a straight shot to City Hall. Actually, they rented two apartments, one being a single and the other a double. Margaret had two large bedrooms, a bath, nice size living room and a small kitchen in the one apartment. They had a doorway cut into the next apartment, making a nice size dining room out of what would have been a bedroom. The living-dining area of that apartment became known as Roe's "Boar's Nest." It was his office-bedroom. He had his own bath and his private kitchen, which he kept well stocked with canned drinks, cheeses from all over the world (even some hanging up), a variety of crackers, plenty of junk food, and ice cream in his freezer. This pleased Roe and, of course, it gave Margaret plenty of room for good nourishing food in her kitchen.

Each had their own front door, which was a blessing. Roe would have conferences until late in the night and would want to sleep in a bit, if possible. Margaret had P.E.O. meetings, church circle and other meetings, and these did not disturb Roe. It was really a beautiful arrangement for these two busy people.

During most of their life in Kansas City, Margaret and Roe had a silent or private telephone number, but Roe had told Margaret he felt it was his duty for them to have a published number. Never did they dream of all the phone calls they would receive. They got calls about everything at all hours ... calls about people having their water turned off, sewer trouble, animal control, trash not being picked up, whatever! Margaret always turned the phone off at night by Roe's bed; therefore she was the one who got all the calls and resulting lack of sleep. It was soon decided they would again have a silent number on the homefront. In time, a second phone line and number was put in the " Boar's Nest," making it possible for Roe to have a private business line, leaving the other to Margaret for all her personal business. Either or both could be turned off at night, if necessary, for a decent night's sleep. This was before answering machines.

Margaret thoroughly enjoyed the duties Roe delegated to her. She loved being in the public eye, and having been on the stage for years, she was used to an audience and had no trouble speaking. She was indeed thrilled when a group wanted a key to the city presented to their out-of-town speaker and Roe would inform them he had a previous commitment but would be happy to send one of the councilmen. The reply coming back was if Roe could not make it, they did not want a councilman, they preferred "Miss Maggie." That really helped her ego, and Roe had a sense of pride there as well.

A delegation of mayors from South America came to Kansas City for a three-day session. When they were presented in the arena at the Music Hall, Roe had an officer stationed at Fort Leavenworth from their country to accompany them to the platform. It was a very colorful event. A gentleman came to the box where Margaret was sitting, informing her she was to go back stage as she was to be presented with roses by the head of the group. Margaret had some tall thinking to do in the next 10 minutes, as she wanted to thank them in Spanish, as she knew several did not speak English. She really surprised the audience, Roe and the South Americans by thanking them in Spanish. She got a big hand from one and all.

One of the greatest thrills for Margaret was when the vice-president of Brazil and his beautiful wife, Theresa, were in Kansas City for four days. Margaret was told the wife did not speak English so Margaret studied up on her Spanish several days before their arrival. Roe told her she was wasting her time, as Brazilians spoke Portuguese. Margaret knew it, too, but she also knew they spoke Spanish. The two women had a great time together. By the second day, Margaret was thinking in Spanish. She took her guests shopping, as well as to luncheons, dinners and other places that had been set up before their arrival.

Margaret had all kinds of interviews on TV, with Bea Johnson, Randall Jessee, Postmaster General, along with many honored guests. She always welcomed the 4-H girls for the Woman's Chamber during their stay in the city the week before the American Royal. Roe always welcomed the boys, having done so in the past. He continued this until his death. Margaret welcomed many conventions such as the American Business Women's Association, Missouri State Parliamentary Convention, National Catholic Theatre, Regional Children's Theatre, plus many men's organizations.

A request of a different nature came. She was asked to care for Joel McCrea's two sons. They were handsome boys, a little spoiled and full of mischief, but Margaret and they managed to get through the day in good shape.

Life was never dull. The city records prove the hectic life Roe had. He went to every fire that was over a two-alarm; in fact, he had his own fireman slicker, hat and boots. He wore his Kansas City Athletics jacket to the ball games, and he and Margaret hardly missed a game when the team played at the Municipal Ball Field. They attended many parties there, often visiting with the Trumans — Miss Bess was also a baseball fan.

Roe contacted Lamar Hunt in regard to bringing a professional football team to Kansas City. Hunt said he would come and look the situation over, but he would have to come incognito. It was decided he would be called Mr. Lamar; thus, if Roe forgot and called him Lamar, no one would be suspicious. As the whole world knows, Lamar Hunt moved his team to Kansas City, and when it came time to name the team, someone said, "The Chief got us here, so why don't we just become the Kansas City Chiefs?" All agreed and Roe could not have been more pleased. When the team became World Champions, words cannot express the deep feelings, thrill and excitement that went through the Bartle-Taylor clan. No one could have been more proud of the Kansas City Chiefs than Roe.

Family Changes

June 13, 1955, brought forth the last of the Bartle grandchildren. The whole family could hardly believe the news: another girl, a fourth daughter, a precious baby girl named Lynnda. Roe was teased a bit about all these granddaughters, but his reply was he had brought up marvelous Scouts, they needed wives and mothers of their children; therefore he was helping along that line. Margaret always felt it was wonderful, as Roe was with men and boys throughout his life. He adored Jimmy, his tomboy, and now he had three granddaughters to love, cherish and spoil a bit, when Jimmy would let him.

Everyone was terribly busy as a new year dawned. Roe was on a goodwill trip to South America; Margaret was out of town; Jim Taylor was sent on his birthday, February 2, 1956 by Spencer Chemical Company, to set up an office in Fort Worth, Texas, and Jimmy was home holding the fort with her three girls. She cancelled the birthday party for Jim and awaited word from him as to his return home. At the end of February, Jim called and asked Jimmy if she would like to move to Fort Worth. She informed him she was packed, and when would they move? Jimmy met Roe upon his return to Kansas City and broke the news to him the Taylors were moving to Texas.

He had mixed feelings over this news. He was delighted for Jim, but he hated to see his little family move so far away. Jimmy told him he would just have to get more speaking engagements down that way and stop over for a visit — which he often did.

Margaret was completely shocked when she got home to find they would be moving. Jimmy, however, asked her to take care of the girls for a week while she went to Texas to look for a place to live. A wild week of searching for what they wanted turned into two weeks. Finally they purchased a lot in the Ridglea Hills area of Fort Worth and contracted to build the house Jimmy was designing. They rented an apartment close by for them to reside in until the house was finished.

Upon returning to Kansas City, Jimmy had to get everything taken care of as far as the move was concerned. Roe told her he would sell their property for them, so she and the girls could get settled in Texas. When Jim came back to the city, Margaret had a farewell party for them. Like all farewell parties, it was wonderful, and yet sad. Margaret and Roe bid their little family goodbye, watching Jim drive his station wagon out of the driveway with his wife, two little girls, a baby, collie dog and a cat. Jim told them they would take two days to get to Fort Worth, as he was driving down through Arkansas, and with this crew he knew he would be making many stops along the way. The minute they arrived in Fort Worth, they called to inform the folks they had an interesting, beautiful and safe trip.

With this void in their lives, Margaret and Roe were very thankful to keep more than busy. They, as well as Jimmy, in many respects were thankful the family had moved out of the Kansas City area. The Greenlease boy had been kidnapped and a car dealer's wife kidnapped, the results being death for both. Margaret and Roe never really knew how Jimmy felt, but she was afraid for her children and was thankful to move out of the territory. They could live a life of their own and not be expected to perform official duties. Margaret and Roe had let the children cut ribbons for the opening of many businesses, sit in the lead cars at parades and other functions, so it was a relief to get away from it all and bring the children up in a normal family life.

Roe was on KMBC radio every morning at 8 a.m. telling about the latest happenings in the city. Some mornings were rather hectic, especially when he had been out until the wee hours the previous night. Margaret would call Torrey Southwick at the station to tell him Roe was on his way, as many times it would be 8:30 before he would arrive.

Roe ran for mayor for a second term and won again. The first four years were the more enjoyable for him. During the second term there were councilmen who voted against everything. This very much disturbed him. Margaret really worried, as Roe would walk the floor at night and kept asking himself, "What can I do? They are ruining my city." There were five councilmen having private meetings (which were illegal), in which they were deciding what they were going to do and how they would vote.

When it came time for a third term, Roe was asked to run again. He had given the citizens of Kansas City over eight years of his undivided attention, striving to do what was best for one and all. He was on the ticket, but begged people to vote for another candidate, as he really did not want the honor for another four years. He received many votes but was greatly relieved when he lost the election.

Three Charmers

Pamela, being the oldest, got to do more than the other girls. One thing she loved was when Donald, the city chauffeur, picked her up to take her to City Hall for a special ribbon cutting. Along the way, she would have him stop at a special drugstore for an ice cream cone, plus coloring books, crayons and the like. She always told him her Gran Gran said it was okay, and he was supposed to buy these things for her. Donald complied, and Roe always got a big kick out of how this little gal wangled her way through for her wants and desires.

Margaret had Sandy assist her on several public occasions. She always felt very grown up and was excited to help her Granny Girl.

Margaret wanted to go back to Kentucky to visit her family and asked to take Pam and Sandy. The girls were delighted with the news they would be going with Granny Girl. Margaret drove, as she had so many towns to visit and people to see. She wanted to be free to do as she saw fit since she did not know how the girls would behave on the trip. All three, however, had a wonderful visit with everyone. The girls had many cousins to play with, new Southern foods to try, and learned a great deal about country living while they were gone.

Roe wanted to send Pam to a camp in Colorado. Jimmy and Jim talked it over, consented and put Pam on the train to Denver. There were many other campers aboard, and these with others transferred to a bus to Camp Sylvania of the Rockies near Bailey, Colorado. The camping session was for eight weeks, and Pam had a marvelous experience. She particularly enjoyed riflery and learning to ride Arabian horses. At the end of the

Gran Gran taking Pam and Sandy to lunch at the Kansas City Club.

eight weeks, all the campers had a part in one of the great Broadway productions. The orchestra was comprised of campers with their own musical instruments, and those with the best singing voices were in parts or chorus. The youngest ones were included and usually stole the show. All parents and grandparents in attendance thoroughly enjoyed the evening with pride. The following year, Sandy joined Pam for the eight weeks of camping. When Lynnda turned five, she joined her sisters at Sylvania, and cried when it was time to return home to Texas.

Jimmy and Jim took advantage of the girls' absence with Jimmy accompanying Jim most of the summer while he covered his territory in New Mexico, Oklahoma, west Louisiana and most of Texas. The summer all three girls were in camp, Jimmy spent the whole eight weeks working up and completing each daughter's photo and scrapbook albums, a huge task.

Pam had just finished her junior year of high school and was setting up courses for the senior year, when the counselor told her she had not yet taken American history and would have to take it along with American government and Texas history the following year. This was overpowering, and she came home very upset. After discussing the situation and finding she could take American history at some other school during the summer months, it was decided she would attend Southwest High School in Kansas City, Missouri. Granny Girl and Gran Gran were overjoyed and delighted to have her for the summer. It was an eight-week course for four hours each morning. Pam thoroughly enjoyed her studies that summer and was able to contribute much that had come to her through history from the Roe side of the family. Margaret chauffeured her to and from school, and then they had luncheons and fun times in the afternoons. The evenings were set aside for study, except those involving season tickets for Starlight Theatre performances.

It was difficult for the Taylor family to go to Kansas City for the Christmas holiday season. Jim would have to take vacation time to do so, and this, of course, cut summer vacation time short, but they did it. Five people popping into the Plaza House seemed like an army had arrived. Upon their departure, Roe would tell Jim, "The freezer was full upon your arrival, and now it is empty again. I don't see how you can afford to feed those three growing girls."

Jim informed him, "It is not easy." There were, however, a few Christmas holidays that found Margaret and Roe in Texas. Often Roe would have meetings in Dallas, Fort Worth or Houston, and Margaret would stay with the family, and Roe would be with them as frequently as possible.

Roe did have many speaking engagements in the state of Texas, and whenever he made it to Fort Worth, excitement followed on Shannon Drive. Other times, Roe would call Jimmy from the Kansas City airport, telling her he would be at Dallas Love Field or DFW Airport for a 30-minute layover and, if possible, would love seeing the family. Jimmy would get the girls in the house, grab a wet wash cloth and towel, pile one and all in the station wagon, and take off. They would wipe their face and hands and comb their hair while Jimmy sped on to the airport. Often they would arrive, dashing to the gate, to find Roe standing there waiting and wondering where they had been. After the short visit, they would make the hour-long drive back home. Down through the years, they never missed a chance of making this trip.

Whether for 15 minutes or for an hour, it was worth every moment.

Pam set a February date for her wedding. She was advised, weatherwise, that was the worst month for Texas. February arrived with blizzards, sleet, snow and freezing weather throughout the central and eastern sections of the United States. Three of her bridesmaids were not able to leave their homes. Flights all over the country were cancelled, and transportation was at a standstill. Roe and Margaret got out on the last flight that left Kansas City. A basketball team with all their gear filled that flight. Upon arrival, Margaret and Roe discovered their luggage had not arrived with the flight. Margaret was really disturbed. She certainly did not want to wear her travel clothes for the rest of her stay in Fort Worth. All relaxed when the following morning the airline delivered their luggage safely to the door. They never knew if it had been trucked or if another flight managed to fly out of Kansas City early the following morning, arriving safely at DFW Airport.

Roe took part in the wedding service held at First Presbyterian Church in Fort Worth — another cherished memory for the entire family.

Sandy was the first grandchild to graduate from college. Margaret was hoping Roe would be able to attend with her but, per usual, he was speaking at another graduation service. Margaret packed and arrived in Fort Worth for a visit before going with the family to Stephen F. Austin College in east Texas. Margaret had never been in this part of Texas and was surprised to see all the beautiful roses in bloom, huge pine trees and the lush and hilly countryside. Upon arrival, Sandy showed Granny Girl the campus, before she had to report to the auditorium. The family got seated, and when Sandy received her diploma, Jimmy looked at Margaret and saw tears rolling down her cheeks. This was a first, and she was thrilled.

Margaret never finished college, as she had married Roe, and they immediately moved to Wyoming. Jimmy had not finished either, as she got too engrossed in the business world and, of course, after meeting Jim, was more interested in being married. Regarding the third generation, Pam quit college to be married. Sandy, however, was motivated to be a good student and a real achiever in everything she did, so she went on to get her degree.

Margaret and Roe became great-grandparents for the first time on May 29, 1970, when Pam gave birth to a beautiful daughter, Lara. One and all were thrilled, but Roe told Jimmy he could not believe she was a grandmother. Where had the years gone? November 18, 1971, Roe was in the midst of making a speech when he was interrupted. There was a special announcement to be made. Roe was informed he had just become a grandfather to Michael Roe. Roe could hardly believe his ears and let out a loud shout. He was indeed pleased at long last to have a male member added to his family. He cut his speech short so he could get to the phone and call Fort Worth.

When Michael Roe was a month old, his family was transferred to Hamilton, Ohio. It was decided that Pam and the children would first go to Kansas City for a visit, before proceeding to Ohio. They had hardly arrived when Pam had to be rushed to the hospital for a gall bladder operation.

Margaret called Jimmy and said she could take care

of Mike if Jimmy could take care of Lara. It was agreed, and Lara flew back to the Taylors on the following day. Lara was very much excited to get back to Mema and Gran Gran Daddy. Margaret had Pam and Michael Roe for six weeks, then they flew on to Ohio to get settled in their new home. Jimmy and Jim had a lot of fun with Lara, though she was never still for a minute. They kept Lara until the end of May, but managed to get her home to her family in time for her second birthday.

Where Have the Years Gone?

As many have said, to know Roe Bartle you knew three things immediately: he was a Southerner, he was a devout Presbyterian, and he believed every citizen had an obligatory responsibility to the generation which followed. The dominant quality which characterized his life was his faith in the worth of his fellowman.

Through his life he was no stranger to struggle. The poverty of the manse was offset spiritually, but not personally. Hand-me-down clothes were painful to him, as he was overgrown in size. He was a lively and fun-loving youth who found life grim when there was no money in the pocket. Being the son of a preacher in a poor community often bred more rebellion than religion at that time. All these inhibitions produced a self-conscious teenager whom Fork Union Military Academy stirred up. He paid grateful tribute to the philosophy and personality of the school for having taught him to use his God-given assets — an alert mind, a resonant voice, a religious depth, quick adaptability, capacity for vision and a heritage of concern for his fellow man.

Most who knew him had the feeling they were his best friend. He never knew a stranger and never forgot a name. If he met you 10 years ago, he immediately recalled the name upon the next meeting and used it.

For 30 years plus, as a Boy Scout Executive, he advanced his paychecks back to the Boy Scouts of America. His councils were tops. No one could beat his records, and he gave leadership to all youth programs with impartial vigor. He served as a co-founder, board member and president of the Boys' Club of Kansas City. He was founder of the Junior Chamber of Commerce. For 16 years he was national president of Alpha Phi Omega, the Scouting Service Fraternity, with chapters in more than 400 colleges and universities. He was venerated by the Future Farmers of America. He held the Legion of Honor for service to DeMolay. He also assisted Frank Land in the writing of the ritual for DeMolay. In 1948 he was head of the Community Chest Campaign for the agencies of Greater Kansas City. For three years he was chairman of the Jackson County Board of Visitors, battling for improved conditions in the county institutions for the youth and aged.

In the field of education, he served on the boards of religious colleges, osteopathic colleges, the Council for the Advancement of Small Colleges, and headed many college finance campaigns. He served two years as interim president of Missouri Valley College. He was a member of the board for the Council for the Advancement of Colleges.

In 1948 he launched the American Humanics Foundation, one of the dreams of his life. Due to this program, there are hundreds of graduates serving in professional Scouting, YMCA, YWCA, Boys Club, Girls Club, Juvenile

Roe with his friend Harry Truman. Charley Hipsh assisting in the presentation to Harry.

Court and Probation, children's hospitals and homes, corrective institutions, neighborhood centers and many other youth-oriented organizations. Roe felt this was probably his greatest single contribution to America. For many years he donated a greater part of his speech money to help keep this organization financially strong.

He was a very involved and responsible citizen in the business world. He served on the boards of numerous corporations and banks and led Commissions into Latin America regarding trade relations. In sports, he was mainly responsible for bringing both major league baseball and football to Kansas City.

He was a trustee of the Menninger Foundation, three hospitals and two agencies. Simultaneously with all the other responsibilities, he served as a public member of the War Labor Board, as a certified arbitrator of the

American Arbitration Association, and as a member of the Loyalty Board of the United States. As a result of his speaking engagements and publicity, he was Kansas City's number one Goodwill Ambassador.

He was the first friend of all faiths. He filled many a pulpit throughout the year when ministers became ill, were called out of town, or were on vacation. In order to do such, he just needed time to dress and get to the church. He would work his sermon out along the way. He was a ruling elder of the Presbyterian Church of the U.S. He served eight years on the General Council of his denomination and a like term as a member of its Board of Annuities and Relief. He has been honored by Catholics, Hebrews and Protestants of many denominations.

He was a trustee of the Midwest Research Institute, a director of Basic Research Corporation, a member of the Board of Governors of Freedoms Foundation at Valley Forge, member of the Commission on Human Relations, member of the Board of Governors of the American Royal livestock show, director of the President Harry S. Truman Library at Independence, Missouri, and lifetime member in National Association of Deans and Advisors of Men.

He was awarded His Majesty's Medal for Service in the Cause of Freedom by Great Britain, a Commander First Class of the Order of Merit by Ecuador, and a commander of the Order of the Crown by Belgium. Other countries conferring distinguished service medals and awards upon him were the Republic of Chile, Uruguay, Brazil, Venezuela, Peru, Guatemala and Mexico.

Roe was a former president of the Juvenile Improvement Association of Kansas City, Missouri. For three years he was chairman of Jackson County Board of Visitors and served as chairman of Board of Merit of Jackson County's Juvenile Court for eight years.

He was past Commander of the Heart of America Post of the American Legion. He was named by the 24 Legion Posts of Kansas City as Kansas City's Distinguished Citizen and was cited by the Veterans of Foreign Wars in 1935 as Citizen of the Year.

When others have gotten together and talked about this man — Roe Bartle — they have discovered a chain of countless stories testifying to his endless capacity for compassion and courage, through work and watchfulness, through vision and valor, through weariness and struggle, through high hopes and higher goals, through misunderstandings and new beginnings, through honor in purpose and in deed, he always exemplified his faith in the worthiness of man, the key to his pattern of living.

During WWII he was executive director of American War Dads' social welfare group and expanded it from an area organization to a national one, and he never accepted a salary.

He organized the Cumerford, Inc. fund-raising organization. He was a national executive board member of Conference of Christians and Jews.

In his public speaking, he blew out many public speaking systems but never had a problem being heard, as he informed everyone he was wired for sound, and no one had a problem hearing him.

His friend, Harry Truman, personally requested him to be the regional director of Economic Stabilization Agency for Missouri, Iowa, Nebraska and Kansas. He could not refuse the President after having talked for years about citizen responsibility. To accept and fulfill this position, he had to resign from 57 boards, as he could not be affiliated with anything that might have represented a conflict of interest. This was from 1951-52.

He was a Mason, York Rite, Knight of Constantine, Scottish Rite, KCCH, Shriner and Jester. He was a past president of the Downtown Rotary Club when they had about 300 members and often said you can never become president of an organization on a 40-hour week.

As an ambassador for Kansas City, he said, "Our job is to sell the efficient, businesslike, low-tax, forward-striving honesty of Kansas City to manufacturers all over the world and at the same time make our town honest and pure, vitalized by a religious life in which the spirits of men are rekindled. We have thrown aside the swaddling clothes of civic infancy for the full mantle of manhood."

He was founder of the Kansas City Commission for International Relations and Trade.

Roe was an honorary life member of Sertoma International, Optimist International and Kiwanis. He was also a life member of the Advertising and Sales Executive Club of Kansas City, Missouri. He was co-founder of Boys' Club of Kansas City, Missouri.

All of the above-mentioned are but a few of the many boards Roe served as a member, plus being cited by many other organizations from the '30s through the early '70s.

It might be noted the degrees he earned were the Associate of Arts (A.A.), Bachelor of Laws (L.L.B.) and Doctor of Jurisprudence (J.D.). Many honorary degrees were conferred by institutions of higher learning such as Doctor of Laws, Doctor of Humane Letters, Doctor of Science, Doctor of Civil Law and Doctor of Literature.

Roe was elected to the Missouri Academy of Squires. He was also elected to the American Academy of Achievement and was one of a class of 40 to receive the Golden

Plate Award in Salt Lake City on July 6, 1972. Jimmy and Jim were able to be with him for this recognition, and they were honored in being able to meet all the other recipients ... definitely "top drawer."

Roe was one of five individuals who had been selected by the American Legion of the Department of Missouri for the Distinguished Service Award. The awards were presented posthumously to General John J. Pershing and Walt Disney. President Harry Truman and General Omar Bradley were the other two who had received this award.

The American Artificer's Award (the third given) was conferred upon Roe by the Flag Plaza Foundation of Pittsburgh, Pennsylvania.

Roe is the only former mayor having been elected and inaugurated as Mayor Emeritus of the City of Kansas City and to serve for a lifetime.

Roe was made an honorary member citizen of over 450 cities, both domestic and international. Certificates and keys were conferred upon him from around the world.

He was also elected a Fellow in the American College of Philanthropy and Services.

Roe Bartle has known the tear that teaches joy, the pain that teaches mercy, and the loneliness that teaches love. He was always proud of his profession. A champion for the underdog, patient with human needs, yet impatient with those not using their talents to the fullest.

Roe touched the stars in the shining lives of great souls. He was fearless in a fight for the right for honor, country and home. No task was too small nor a challenge too great. His constant mission in life was to give of himself with a prayer always for others. He was kind, yet tough; proud but humble; robust, although possessed with a fragile soul. His helping mankind came from a sense of love for his fellow men rather than duty. He was so human in his common touch that a waitress became a duchess, a janitor a king, and a President a buddy.

And finally ... one of Roe's favorite quotes was from Webster:

> *If you work upon marble, it will perish;*
> *If you work upon brass, time will efface it;*
> *If you build temples, they will crumble into dust;*
> *But if you work upon the immortal soul of men,*
> *Give them a just fear of God*
> *And cause them to love their fellow men,*
> *You engrave upon those tablets something*
> *That will last through all eternity.*
> *He did that kind of work.*

Margaret kept active in the three amateur theatrical groups and nine civic organizations, but a great expanse of her time was consumed in aiding and assisting Roe.

She often said of Roe, "Papa can do anything on this earth that he sets out to do. I have seen him accomplish the impossible, and he has more energy than any other five men alive. I have said for years that my husband would make as fine a President as these United States has ever had."

Half Century Mark

Roe had been having his ups and downs healthwise for several years. He had pushed and pushed his body for too many years without adequate rest or concern for himself.

Jimmy made numerous trips to Kansas City to visit

with him when he was ill. Each time it seemed to revitalize him, and he was soon up and out again. She knew the day would come when the transfer of energy would not work, but tried to never think about that.

September 26, 1973, arrived with Roe once again in the hospital. All of the 50th wedding anniversary party plans were set aside. It was a great disappointment for all. Jimmy had mentioned since there would be no reception for them, it was a plus there would be no one with hurt feelings because they might not have been invited. Jimmy had informed her parents she could not afford to invite the whole city of Kansas City for their 50th!

Jimmy and the girls called Roe during the afternoon. Even in the hospital it was hard getting to talk to him. Margaret was on hand, so she did most of the talking to the Texas crew, as Roe was being interviewed on TV. The anniversary package from the Taylor clan arrived while they were on the phone so, of course, it was opened to reveal an eight-place setting of gold flatware. The folks were thrilled, but most importantly, they had each other and had made it to their 50th.

October and November found Margaret making two trips to the hospital with bulbar pneumonia. Roe was being nursed at home and kept Jimmy informed via Ma Bell.

Jimmy decided to go to Kansas City for Thanksgiving, as Margaret was back home and the three of them could have their own holiday celebration. Dr. Arnold Arms came by each day checking on them and apologized to Jimmy that her folks could not leave the apartment to eat out, and it was her birthday. Jimmy replied to the doctor that it was a great birthday as she had both of her parents back under the same roof and off the seriously ill list, and that made for a wonderful birthday.

Being Thanksgiving time also, she felt she had much to be thankful for and many prayers had been answered.

Roe was feeling so much better than he expressed the desire to return to Virginia one more time. He wanted to drive and have a leisurely type trip. Dr. Arms informed him that would be nice come spring, as long as he had a driver and he would only be a passenger. That was agreed upon. Lynnda got ear of her Gran Gran's wishes and discussed it with the family and received permission to be his chauffeur if the plans could be carried out. She remained out of college that semester so she would be available to leave for Virginia on short notice. It was always a great disappointment to her the trip was never made. Nonetheless, Roe was very appreciative of her willingness to assist and her desire to always help make him happy.

Dr. Arms asked Jimmy if she could take her mother back to Texas where she could spend the winter in a warmer climate. With no hesitation and a big smile, she replied, "It would be a pleasure." Both Margaret and Jimmy hated to leave Roe behind, but he preferred to remain in Kansas City, and proper arrangements to care for him were made before they headed south. It was a fun trip to Fort Worth, and the excited clan met them at the door full of hugs, kisses and chatter.

It was a very strange Christmas holiday that year. Roe did not feel well enough to travel to Texas. He therefore remained in Kansas City and planned for his Christmas Day. He visited the jail, boys' home and other such places during the morning hours, then celebrated with his "holiday family." He set up a lovely dinner at the Kansas City Club for his friends who were without family and purchased gifts for all in attendance. That sort of day always gave him a satisfied feeling.

In Texas, Margaret had a busy holiday season with the Taylor family. They, too, had all their family plus friends who were alone for the holidays. That had been a tradition carried out each year.

Margaret had a warm reception everywhere she went, which made her feel very much more at home while in Fort Worth. Jimmy and Jim's friends invited her to everything, and many called just to visit with her over the phone. Roe called her several times a week to check on how she was feeling. She was getting stronger with each passing day and was having such a good time she did not want to go home, but she did not mention this to Roe.

Roe's last official outing was breaking ground for the convention hall soon to be built. He was deeply touched, greatly moved and deeply honored, as he felt this was recognition from all the citizens of Kansas City. No man can be honored more than by his own people. It was like an impossible dream come true. What a beautiful way to close a final chapter of his book of life. Jimmy was so thankful all this came about while he was living, for it was far more meaningful to the family and friends than doing such after his death.

Roe had secretly hoped the day might arrive when the Osceola Scout Camp might bear his name but never dreamed it would truly happen, especially in his lifetime. What a thrill for that dream to come true! All "his boys" and the people of "his city" had paid him the highest of tributes, and he was indeed grateful.

Jimmy realized during phone calls in March, Roe was not feeling up to par. She informed Margaret, as much as she would like to keep her longer, she now felt it was her place to get back to Kansas City and tend to Roe.

Margaret flew home the middle of March, found Roe ill, and two days later she entered him in St. Luke's Hospital. His visit to the hospital this time was serious, and few visitors were allowed. Jimmy told Margaret and the doctor if they took Roe's public away, he too would fade away.

May 8, 1974, Dr. Arms called Jimmy at 4 p.m., telling her he and Roe had had a long talk. Roe was tired of fighting all the pain he had suffered for years and felt it was time to let go. Therefore Dr. Arms informed Jimmy she had best plan on coming up shortly, as patients do not last long once they have surrendered. Jimmy immediately made plans to fly out the following morning at 9:30. She located Jim, he packed up and returned to Fort Worth, and she made arrangements for family and pets while out of town. With everything finally under control and Jim having arrived home in good shape, she dropped into bed at 2:45 a.m.

At 3:30 a.m. that same night, May 9, 1974, the phone rang in Fort Worth. Jimmy answered the phone softly, and upon hearing her mother's voice, she interrupted, saying, "I didn't make it, did I?" Margaret told her Roe passed away peacefully at 3 a.m., and she wanted to wait until she got home to call. Jimmy told her she would call the airline and secure a ticket for Jim, hopefully on the same flight, so they could arrive at the same time, and she would plan her dad's funeral upon arrival, which pleased Margaret. Jimmy contacted her three daughters, and arrangements were made for them to meet and drive up together.

Margaret met Jimmy and Jim at the airport, and on the way to the funeral home the majority of plans were well discussed and soon put into motion. They relaxed when the girls finally arrived on the scene. They really had to pedal to arrive in time for the Mic-O-Say service that evening.

Family and friends from all over the United States arrived in Kansas City. Many of the Scouters attending a conference in Hawaii came for the service and returned to the islands for the rest of the conference. Friends from all walks of life, all faiths, all colors, overflowed Central Presbyterian Church to honor this man who had befriended them through the years. Four men of the cloth spoke on his behalf, and his favorite hymns were sung by a young couple from the opera company, accompanied by Barry Richardson. It was a most memorable service.

Riding to the cemetery, all who were on the street and sidewalks stopped and saluted; men removed their hats; many crossed themselves. It might be said the citizens Roe worked so diligently for were showing their appreciation, respect and thanks and were bidding him farewell. The most impressive and unforgettable scene occurred when the cars entered the gates of Forest Hill Cemetery. From the gates to the gravesite, the way was completely lined with Cub Scouts, den mothers, Boy Scouts and Scouters. They had been waiting for hours to honor their Chief. Their extended warmth and love was a great comfort. Roe's last journey was by six firemen and six policemen chosen to be pallbearers. They proudly carried the Chief to the gravesite, and the family was grateful and proud of them.

Roe and Jimmy had had a remarkable talk back in November before she took her mother to Texas. At that time he informed her, "Have no regrets when my time comes. I have lived life in the manner I desired." They each told the other just what they thought of their lives, the good and the bad, and their feelings for each other.

It was a treasured visit and gave Jimmy a feeling of satisfaction and peace.

It was Mother's Day weekend. Dianne had been buried on the Saturday before Mother's Day, and now so was Roe. Margaret felt fortunate, in the years ahead, if she managed to make it past Mother's Day. She would say she must be good for another year.

Family and friends left the city during the following few days. Margaret's youngest sister, Anna Mae, stayed on to help, and Jimmy remained to assist Margaret with Roe's estate. It took her three months to shut down the "Boar's Nest." Numerous boxes were catalogued and labeled for storage. Donation of his papers, books, personal belongings and other memorabilia were donated to numerous colleges, historical societies, Boy Scouts, Mic-O-Say, Alpha Phi Omega, Mayor's office and Council of the City of Kansas City, American Humanics, personal friends and family. All did their best to comply with each request. Roe shared himself in life, and they were doing their best to keep on sharing. Roe always said he gave his body the mileage of 10 men and loved every mile of it.

Jimmy's wish was that his memory live on in the lives of those whom he knew, worked with, and touched in so many fields during his life, and that the great architectural structure of Bartle Hall with his statue and an exhibit would bring forth a curiosity from youth and newcomers to the city, so they would reach out to learn more about the man for whom the center was named — proving what one man can accomplish in a lifetime in this great country we live in.

While Jimmy and Anna Mae were with Margaret, she got many things accomplished, even redecorating the apartment and shutting down the Boar's Nest, which was

The official portrait of Mayor Bartle

soon rented as an efficiency apartment. By the time her sister and daughter returned to their respective homes, Margaret was ready to get back into the busy stream of living.

Roe's Miss Maggie in the 1940s

Roe's Miss Maggie

Roe's Miss Maggie came forth unfolding in full bloom, showing the citizens of Kansas City the real woman who was behind Roe through all those busy years.

For many, many years, Roe always referred to Margaret as "Miss Maggie" in his speeches. She never really liked being called "Maggie," but after all the wonderful letters she received after Roe's demise where practically everyone referred to her as Miss Maggie, at long last she felt it was an endearing title. Those who called her that always received a big smile, and there would be a twinkle in her eye.

Her calendar was fully booked. Jimmy would call from 8 a.m. until midnight, with no answer. When she would finally catch her, Margaret would inform her she had been home several times to change clothes, and tell her the happenings of the day. By this time she was past president of Community Children's Theatre, Kansas City Women's Association of International Relations and Trade, and Chapter CF, P.E.O. Sisterhood. She was a life member of Kansas City Young Matrons and the Kansas City Rose Society. She was a charter member of Wives of Rotarians and was a trustee of the American Humanics Foundation. She was still most active in Saddle and Sirloin Club, the Elizabeth Benton Chapter of the Daughters of the American Revolution, the Kansas City Museum, Women's City Club, Kansas City Athenaeum, Delta Phi Chapter of Alpha Delta Pi Sorority, the Rehabilitation Institute and the Salvation Army. She was an honorary director of Rockhurst College and Avila College, an honorary member of Women's Chamber of Commerce, the American Women's Association, Fraternity Order of Eagles Auxiliary and Beta Sigma Phi Sorority. She was also on several bowling teams.

In her spare time she visited the family, enjoyed her friends, wrote letters and read murder mystery books.

Granddaughter Pam delivered another son on September 12, 1975. Gregory James was born in Milwaukee, Wisconsin. Mema Jimmy left a Model A Ford Club meet in Oklahoma and drove up to Wisconsin to take care of everyone. Two grandsons for her, that was a record, and granddaughter Lara was a big-little helper.

It was a particularly exciting day for the Bartle-Taylor clan when the day arrived for the dedication of Bartle Hall. Jimmy wrote Margaret's speech, which they discussed over the phone many times. Jimmy felt Roe was there, although she was perhaps the only one who felt such. It would be difficult to imagine a more magnificent tribute to a man who had done so much for his favorite city in the entire world. Margaret did a great job, and it was a very memorable occasion.

Felix De Weldon had been commissioned to produce a statue of Roe to be placed in Bartle Hall. He was the sculptor who did the "Raising the Flag Over Iwo Jima." His studio was located in Washington, D.C. When Felix was ready for Margaret and Jimmy to come and approve his clay model, Jimmy flew to Kansas City so she and Margaret could go on the same flight back to the capitol. While there, they stayed with a life-long friend of Margaret's at her 1812 Georgetown home. Their week was most interesting, and Felix was very patient with them. Each day they went to view his work, and each day he was asked to change the nose or the ears, the eyes or forehead. It got to be something else. Finally when Margaret and Jimmy were on their flight back to Kansas City, each looked at the other and asked, "Do you think it looks like Dad?" The model had been changed so much, they really could not answer that question truthfully, as it was difficult to detect if this huge amount of molded clay was really true to life. In some ways it seemed rather illusory, and they prayed a lot over what would be the final result of this project.

Time grew near for the dedication of the statue. Once again, Jimmy wrote out a speech for Margaret to deliver. Two evenings before driving to Kansas City for the dedication, Jim took Jimmy out to dinner. Walking back to their car, Jim went ahead to unlock the vehicle, and Jimmy fell into a hole in the parking lot, breaking her ankle. The evening was spent in the emergency ward, but there was no way anyone could keep her in the hospital. She was going to Kansas City, no matter what! Jim drove to Kansas City with Jimmy sitting in the back seat with her leg up on the front arm rest all 550 miles. She had never been on crutches before, and that was a real challenge — the pits. She was not going to let anything stop her from attending the dedication. She made it in good shape, and Margaret delivered her talk like a pro. Yes, it was decided at one special angle, the statue really did look like Roe. They were told earlier by Felix that Roe would not be rotund, as he wanted the statue to show strength and power. It was interesting to hear the various remarks throughout the crowd regarding the unveiled work of art.

Margaret enjoyed her trips with the Women's Commission to Kansas City's sister city. She loved to travel and was always delighted to be able to present keys to her city to heads of state and other dignitaries. She was called upon by many mayors of Kansas City to present the honored key when their schedule would not permit them to do so. She felt it was always wonderful to be remembered, as well as needed and to be helpful. She used her Spanish at every opportunity, which always surprised and impressed the visitors to the city from south of the border.

Margaret felt Bartle Hall needed exhibit cases for Roe's memorabilia to give the public a better understanding of the man called Chief Roe Bartle. The city did not have funds for such; therefore, Sidney Willens, one of Roe's boys, started the ball rolling. He wrote letters by the dozens, spoke on radio and TV. He worked tirelessly on this project that he knew was Miss Maggie's dream and focus in life. She mailed out hundreds of letters explaining her hopes and requesting contributions for the project. She worked tirelessly to achieve this burning desire.

On August 15, 1985, Jimmy went with Jim to Waco, Texas, on business. While Jim was making calls, Jimmy shopped at the big new mall. They met at the mall for lunch, and while there made place and time arrangements to meet at 5 p.m. for the trip back to Fort Worth. Jim returned to the mall to pick Jimmy up and, not finding her, inquired at security and asked them to page her. After finding out who he was, they informed him his wife had been taken to Providence Hospital, but was okay. The truth was, however, they thought she had expired. Jim arrived at the hospital and learned his wife was in surgery, as she had experienced a serious heart attack, with 95 percent blockage. He notified his Fort Worth family, then called Margaret, but told her to sit tight and he would keep her informed as he learned more of Jimmy's situation and progress. This was a real shocker for the whole family — Jimmy, too!

A week later, Jim brought Jimmy home in a friend's van, as he felt she would be far more comfortable stretched out a bit. It was great getting home, where she took it easy as long as she could; then she had to get busy as time was drawing near for things to be finalized for her daughter's wedding. Margaret came down for all the festivities and excitement. Lynnda married Michael John Burroughs on October 26, 1985, in Fort Worth at Ridglea Presbyterian Church. Everything went off beautifully as planned. The newlyweds went to Hawaii, and the rest of the family had a good visit over the weekend, and life was soon back to normal.

After graduation, Sandy became a speech pathologist in Corpus Christi during the winter months and director of Girl Scout Camp Texlake on Lake Travis near Austin, Texas, during the summer. She had been involved in Girl Scouting since the second grade. She was president of Senior Planning Board, went to the Girl Scout Cabana in Mexico and was selected for trips to national events. At one point she taught counselor-in-training, and that was the year Lynnda sold the most Girl Scout cookies in the Council and was awarded any session in camp she wished. She chose to get her counselor-in-training, which made it a little rough on both girls. Sandy gave up her teaching job and worked full-time for the Lone Star Girl Scout Council, headquartered in Austin, Texas. After seven years she accepted a position with the regional office in Dallas. When national closed down the regional office, she applied and was hired as a management consultant in the New York National Girl Scout office. That was a rather stressful job, as her territory was Alaska, Montana, California, Nevada, North Dakota, Wyoming and Oregon. She learned there was an opening for executive director of Girl Scouts Wagon Wheel Council in Colorado Springs, Colorado, applied, was interviewed, called back several times, and was picked for the position. Another big move, a big challenge, and like her grandfather, she gave it her all. Roe may have had just granddaughters, but this granddaughter was carrying on the Scouting tradition in fine fashion and full force through Girl Scouting.

January 19, 1987, saw the arrival of Clayton Taylor Burroughs. Lynnda had had problems in the previous months; therefore Margaret was very relieved when she got word the young man had arrived, and Lynnda was doing okay. She had two sons to look after now, as she had a teenage stepson, Timothy Jon. Margaret and Jimmy could not help but remark, it was a pity Roe could not have lived to see and know all his grandsons.

Lynnda asked Granny Girl if she would please come down for Clayton's christening and spend some time with the family. Margaret looked her calendar over and felt she could make it but would not be able to stay over too

Margaret presented the keys to the city to many distinguished visitors including Liberace (right) and his brother.

long. Margaret arrived a few days ahead of time and was a great help to Jimmy in that after the christening she had an open house in Clayton's honor. And so Margaret could visit again with her many Fort Worth friends. Margaret thought the table looked terrific, filled with all the fresh fruits, relishes, tea sandwiches, chips 'n' dip and yummy punch. She had a marvelous time, and all were thankful she could be with us.

Margaret returned to Kansas City and entered the hospital for some testing. She did not tell the family of this little trip. The doctors found nothing, yet were puzzled over the way she felt. She decided the best thing to do was pack, attend the American Humanics meeting in Colorado, and forget her pain.

October rolled around. Margaret called Jimmy and said she was entering the hospital again. That was the first that Jimmy knew of the earlier visit. The doctors decided they wanted to do an exploratory on her. Jimmy wanted to fly up immediately, but Margaret said there was no need for that; she would be home in a few days and would have a nice long conversation at that time. She wanted no phone calls or flowers while there. It was hard for Jimmy to comply with those requests.

Two days later, Jimmy received a call from Margaret's surgeon. She was informed that Margaret had cancer of the uterus, and he felt she would only last about two weeks. She could not believe what she was hearing and asked the doctor to repeat what he had said to her. Needless to say, this was a total shock. She knew Margaret had been in pain and had gained weight around the waist rather rapidly but was certainly not ready to hear what she was now hearing. She felt so helpless and could not imagine this woman who had always been a bundle of pep and energy was now lying in the hospital alone.

Jimmy contacted all the members of her family about the situation. It was decided that Lynnda, Clayton and Jimmy would drive up together, and they arrived the following afternoon. Clayton was the best little traveler, sitting in his car seat in the back and sleeping a good bit of the way. Several times they stopped to feed him and let him crawl around to use up some of his energy.

As soon as the car was unloaded, Jimmy went straight to the hospital and surprised Margaret. She was deeply grateful to see her and asked if the doctor had told her of the prognosis. At that point they hugged each other and had a good cry together. Jimmy tried to tell her she was strong and could whip this. They both wanted to make a liar out of the doctor. Jimmy told her mother she had a surprise for her, but she would have to wait until evening. The sparkle returned to Margaret's eyes when Lynnda walked into the room with Clayton in her arms. What a boost for Margaret, and what a charmer Clayton turned out to be.

Margaret had made up her mind she was going to remain in the hospital, but after two days, Jimmy informed Margaret she was going home to the Plaza House where she and Lynnda would take care of her. Margaret did not want to leave the hospital, but found herself in an ambulance heading for home. She remained upset with Jimmy for a couple of days, then called her into her room and thanked her very much for having brought her home. The daughter was right rather than the mother this time. At the hospital people were in and out all day long, the phone rang often, and she was exhausted. Now she felt more relaxed, saw only people she felt like seeing, and had very few phone conversations.

Margaret's sister, Anna Mae, again came from Kentucky to help care for Margaret. Thanksgiving was soon to arrive, as was Jimmy's birthday. The whole Taylor clan was on hand for the holiday weekend. They all stayed at the Plaza House, giving Margaret a chance to have individual visits with her family members. She had told Jimmy of jewelry and certain articles she wanted the various girls to have, and Jimmy convinced her to present these things during their private visits with her, as it would mean so much more receiving them from her than with Jimmy just giving them the items later. Those little visits were marvelous for both parties. They laughed and cried together, plus talking over good times.

Jim knew there was no way Jimmy could prepare a full Thanksgiving dinner for all the crew with everything else she had to do. Therefore it was decided half would go out to eat, then the other half could go. Jim would take the first half, and Jimmy could take the second. What a joke it turned out to be, as he could find nothing open. Places were closed for the day or had finished serving for the day. They came back still starved. Jim wanted to know what he should do or could do. Jimmy laughed and told them she would have a meal for them, a different type meal for Thanksgiving, but one they would truly be thankful to have. Lorraine Willens had brought about two gallons of her super chicken soup the day before, and that turned out to be Thanksgiving dinner for the whole clan. It was marvelous, filling and nourishing, too. There were no complaints.

Bud Keller's birthday was also the 27th of November. His wife, Sydney, invited Jimmy and Jim to join them for lunch at the club. With the rest of the family on hand to see about Margaret, Jimmy decided she could take time out to celebrate her birthday. It was a nice break, delicious lunch and great fellowship. She was very grateful, and also thanked the good Lord for letting her have her mother for one more birthday.

Things settled down after most of the family left. Margaret so enjoyed seeing and visiting with all of them, but cried as they left, as she knew she would not be seeing them again.

Anna Mae stayed up with Margaret at night and would let Jimmy sleep a few hours if possible. Then come morning she would go to bed and Jimmy would take over. There were a select few Jimmy would call on to relieve her during the day to go to the hospital for necessary drugs or to dash to the grocery store for a few items.

On December 7, Jimmy invited Margaret's good friend and traveling buddy, Elizabeth Haynes, to come eat dinner with them. When she arrived, she suggested that she would visit with Margaret and let us eat, and when we had finished, she would eat. She did not want Margaret left alone a minute. Anna Mae and Jimmy were nearly finished with their meal when Elizabeth came into the dining room and told them we had better get back to the bedroom quickly as she felt Margaret was leaving us. Jimmy ran back, trying to talk to Margaret, telling her she loved her and hoped she had a pleasant trip. Within five minutes Margaret was gone, oh, so peacefully.

My, how thrilled she would have been to have seen the packed Central Presbyterian Church on December 11, 1987, for her memorial service, as the family had held a private service that morning at Forest Hill. Jimmy thoroughly enjoyed welcoming everyone at the reception afterward and introducing her family to all in attendance. Indeed, this pair, oh so different, but oh so wonderful and full of talent in their own way were finally gone from this earth, but they definitely left their mark and much for all to live up to. Jimmy, with the help of all her family, packed up all of Margaret and Roe's belongings and took everything to Texas.

It is hoped they inspired those left behind, for they are definitely shoes it will be hard to fill. It is difficult to find such dedicated people in this world today. They were big in heart, keen of mind and willingness of spirit, people of vision, courage, determination and perseverance, who were built solidly and built well.

Life Goes On

Just because Margaret and Roe were gone from this earth was no sign Sidney, Jimmy and others were going to give up on the exhibit cases for Bartle Hall.

Dreams do come true, as we have heard in the past, but even after death, they do. Perseverance does pay off. In November 1989, the unveiling of the exhibit cases for Roe's memorabilia took place. The boxes Jimmy had packed and labeled back in 1974, plus what she had on the homefront, and two years of searching and contributing provided the items to choose for the exhibit cases. Once again it was an exciting day for the Bartle-Taylor clan. Jimmy was thrilled to speak on behalf of the Bartle family for this marvelous display. Margaret would have been pleased and proud, as would have Roe. Jimmy told those present — don't worry; they are among us in one fashion or another, and the Bartle-Taylor clan are most appreciative and deeply humble for the honors extended their family.

Jimmy remembered what her father had taught her:

Know the tear that teaches joy,
The pain that teaches mercy,
The loneliness that teaches love;
Touch the stars in the shining lives of great souls;
Be fearless in a fight for the rights of honor, home
*   and country.*
No task can be too small nor a challenge too great;
Let your constant mission in life be to give yourself away
With a prayer always for others.
Be kind, yet tough, proud but humble.

Jimmy wanted to carry the torch and follow the path her parents would desire. She has cooperated in every manner possible with all requests presented to her. The Pony Express Council asked her to speak at their annual Scouters banquet, and even before thinking, she replied, "Yes." What a thrill for her. She felt like "Queen for a Day." What a magnificent weekend she had in St. Joseph. She spoke, pouring her heart out and received such a heart-warming reception she was brought to tears. She informed them how her dad had been the speaker of the house, and she was there just to have a visit with them. It was a beautiful evening and one that will never be forgotten.

Since that time, she has made many speeches or talks on numerous subjects and knows Roe would be proud of her efforts.

In July of 1990, Bartle Reservation at Osceola, Missouri, celebrated its 60th anniversary. Many old-timers returned to the camp for a day of celebration. Jimmy was on hand to welcome all in attendance and gave a talk to all the Mic-O-Says that evening. She was extended an invitation to attend a ceremonial which she accepted,

Roe bidding Jimmy farewell on her honeymoon — 1947.

never dreaming this would be a possibility. The evening was like a dream, and she spoke to them through her tears as her heart runneth over. The ovation she received was overwhelming. Jim had traveled with her to the reservation, but due to his health problem remained in bed most of the weekend.

Jimmy very much needed all of this at the time as she had put her husband in the hospital the previous October with viral pneumonia. With no response and many tests, it was discovered that due to 13 blood transfusions he had received back during February of 1987, he ended up HIV positive which, of course, is the virus that eventually leads to AIDS. This was devastating for the whole family, as well as friends. Jim had such beautiful faith and was a very strong individual. He put his life in the hands of God, as he always had, and informed the family the world was not coming to an end. He was active in many organizations — Clerk of the Session and elder of his church, past president of his Rotary Club, past president of the Longhorns, past president of Model A Ford Club, a Mason and Shriner, and always concerned for all mankind.

After a long three-year battle, he died on March 17, 1993. The three strong men in Jimmy's life, Sam Bartle, Roe Bartle and Jim Taylor had met their maker, and she alone is carrying the torch, forging ahead to carry on the traditions and way of life in which she was reared, and is ever ready to share and help her fellow person.

In July 1994, a reunion was held at Bartle Reservation of Mic-O-Say members who were in camp in the late '30s and early '40s, in honor of Eldon Newcomb, who had been director of the Nature Lodge and is now an eminent botanist. A luncheon was held on Friday noon in which

Eldon Newcomb and Bob Hunt were presented two beautiful fur medicine man bonnets. There was a constant flow of memories and much warm fellowship. Much to everyone's delight, Sam Reaves, who would be 100 years old the next month, came strolling in, as did Don Baldwin. It was a heartwarming occasion.

Friday evening found many who had attended the luncheon plus many others had arrived for the "old-timers" reunion at the reservation. Jimmy was asked to come to the council ring that evening. John Modlin picked her up. They arrived in good time, and she was seated inside the ring. The proceedings were very interesting and colorful. She felt privileged to be in attendance. Scout Executive and Chief of the Tribe of Mic-O-Say, David Ross, requested that Jimmy come forth, and she complied. Much to her complete astonishment, she began to hear words she could hardly believe. While completely flabbergasted, she was being inducted into the Tribe of Mic-O-Say and was given the name of Lone Bear Princess. Being a very sentimental person, thoughts flew through her mind of her dad's spirit and of her husband as he had been with her the last time she was at the reservation. The ovation she received was the longest, loudest and most enthusiastic any could remember. Needless to say, she stood there with tears flowing, in complete surprise, joy, happiness and humble pride. Nonetheless, she pulled herself together in order to say a few inspiring words to all within the council ring before returning to her seat in the circle.

All the reunion guests were given tours of the camp on Saturday to see the massive changes that had been made over the passing years. Jimmy and the others ate in the dining hall with the boys. Another great experience was Jimmy teaching the Scouts one of the songs sung at camp when she was a child. The boys loved it and asked her to sing it every chance available. Sunday was visitors/parents day which is always full of activities. At 3 p.m. in their colorful regalia, the Mic-O-Say dancers performed in the hot afternoon sun. For one dance the tribesmen picked members of the audience to perform the Indian Two-Step with them. A young brave came forth and asked Jimmy. She was hot and tired, but could not refuse the young man's request. They did the Indian Two-Step five times around the council ring, and upon completion Jimmy thanked her partner and returned to her seat. She was immediately called upon to say a few words to the boys and their parents — which she did, and followed once again singing the song they had requested. A great chapter of memories was compiled from this one weekend for all in attendance, but especially Jimmy.

Gabriel Ashely was born on August 15, 1994, joining her sister, Heather Nicole, now two and a half, making Jimmy a great grandmother for the second time — much to her delight.

Life goes on, and all the memories become very cherished as the Book of Life is filled.

Jimmy has never tried to walk in her parents' shoes, as she is busy making her own footprints while trying to carry on the Bartle spirit.

About the Author

Jimmy Bartle Taylor is the only child of Roe and Margaret Bartle. After Roe Bartle's death, she received many requests to write a book about her parents.

But she first returned to her home in Fort Worth, Texas to finish raising her family, and assisting with her grandchildren. And still later, she took care of her mother until Margaret's death. After that, Jimmy and her husband traveled the United States and the United Kingdom before Jim became seriously ill. After he died, she decided if the book she had promised to write was going to get written, it was best to get busy and follow through. She hopes everyone will enjoy reading the memories of being raised a Bartle.